THIS BOOK
BELONGS TO:

_____

Birth date:

_____

Birth time:

_____

Birth location:

_____

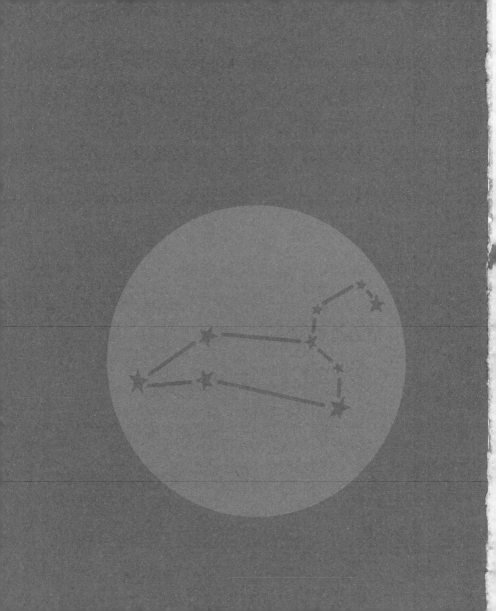

ZODIAC SIGNS

LEO

ZODIAC SIGNS

LEO

BESS MATASSA

STERLING ETHOS
New York

STERLING ETHOS
New York

An Imprint of Sterling Publishing Co., Inc.
1166 Avenue of the Americas
New York, NY 10036

ISBN 978-1-4549-3894-1

Distributed in Canada by Sterling Publishing Co., Inc.
c/o Canadian Manda Group, 664 Annette Street
Toronto, Ontario M6S 2C8, Canada
Distributed in the United Kingdom by GMC Distribution Services
Castle Place, 166 High Street, Lewes, East Sussex BN7 1XU, England
Distributed in Australia by NewSouth Books
University of New South Wales, Sydney, NSW 2052, Australia

For information about custom editions, special sales, and premium
and corporate purchases, please contact Sterling Special Sales at
800-805-5489 or specialsales@sterlingpublishing.com.

Manufactured in China

2 4 6 8 10 9 7 5 3 1

sterlingpublishing.com

Cover design by Elizabeth Mihaltse Lindy
Cover and endpaper illustration by Sarah Frances
Interior design by Nancy Singer
Zodiac signs © wikki33 and macrovector/freepik

To Soulie: My fellow fiery feline floof queen.

And to my Mother: I see your Leo Rising shining through.

CONTENTS

ઈ

INTRODUCTION

Come closer. Put your hands on your own sun-kissed skin and feel the pulsating magenta of the bold blood that courses beneath. The zodiac's "Glitter Kitten" is composed of equal parts fluff and fire, a relentlessly tender sparkler made to sport their pumping heart on ruffled sleeves. Custom-built for a lusty lifetime of recovering and relishing in their own true colors, no matter the cost, Leos are here to show themselves and the world that they were absolutely born to be this way.

Paving the sequined way back to innocence and fueling a thirsty quest for their personal disco balls, these fancy felines are lifelong proclaimers of the message that it is all right to trust this life, exactly as it is. It doesn't mean they'll never get hurt. It doesn't mean they won't want to shut it down, draw the curtains, and throw in the beach towel altogether. In fact, developing some tolerance for the darker shades of experience only makes their glow even glowier, because these summertime astrobabes are ruled by the relentless rise of the scorching sun. Cultivating the willingness to come at it again and again is the magical mission of a lifetime for this warm-blooded cosmic creature, kissing cynicism straight on the lips with cherry balm glitter gloss and a healthy dose of hedonism.

I will love again anyway, says Leo. I will show up at the doorstep of life clad in my finest frocks, regardless of what receives me. I will sport diamonds on the soles of my shoes and glow no matter the weather, pulling the plants out of their dormancy and towards my gorgeous, goddess-given heat. I will open wide to exactly what's here and take it into my heart. I will let myself be moved by the world, so that it will be moved by me.

LEONINE PLEASURE PRINCIPLES

These guiding lights shape the Leonine lifestyle, both as reasons for being and dynamic calls to embrace.

Heat

Signaling the sweat-soaked center of summertime in the Northern Hemisphere, Leo "season" is literally the hottest section of the astrological year (running from late July through the heart of August). As we strip ourselves down to bare skin, shedding our layers and slipping into teeny-weeny swimwear, Leo energy reminds us of the potential seamlessness between our environment and ourselves.

Imagine cocktail hour in the sizzling tropics after an epic day spent frolicking in the hot sun. Whether at high noon or midnight, Leo weather is stable in its temperature. It's connected to its sign's consistency and loyal sense of self-expression. Clad in the same soul clothes no matter the hour, Leos are here to literally close the gap between themselves and the world, reaching out to touch and be touched by the humid air with a delicious sense of reciprocity and a generously seductive availability for exchange.

The second of the fire sign trinity (preceded by engine-revver Aries from late March through April, and followed by wild pony Sagittarius from late November through December), Leo is the roaring beach bonfire to Aries' lit match and Sag's Olympic torch. While the first sign of each element is here for the self (Aries) to initiate and explore, the second is here to "express" that element, collide with the collective, solicit feedback, and divine how to creatively contribute. While the Leonine mission is intensely focused on shining on, no matter what, this sign is also constantly learning how to focus these beams in order to both avoid burnout and best inspire.

In a deep dance with the generous spillage of their one and only selves, Leos' light must also be channeled into coaxing all the little flowers that surround it to burst into full bloom. Leos have literally been incarnated to harness their eternal flames to heat up the world. They must figure out how to share their tropical sensations and contribute to the world without compromising a drop. Think of the energy of a delicate marshmallow roast, where there's both a celebration of toasty open flames and the careful consideration of how to turn all sides golden brown rather than a burnt BBQ. These kittens are here to serve up their signature snacks with honed heat, ensuring that everyone at the bonfire gets to taste the smoky sweetness.

Exposure

Just like how summertime strips away our scratchy layers and brings us back to the beautiful basics of slick skin, Leos are here to work with the principle of "exposure." Contrary to popular belief, this isn't necessarily connected to extroversion. Leos come in all shapes and sizes of loudness and shyness. This process of self-display is less tied to a sense of spectacle than to a willingness to bring whatever part of themselves is most vulnerable to center stage.

Cultivating the capacity to skinny-dip in broad daylight and show themselves no matter what is a constant process of ego rock tumbling that blends unapologetic self-expression with the call to dive deeper into self-awareness. There is an unabashed clarity to the midday sun, which sparkles while illuminating cracks and fissures. Leos are here to bless it all with warmth. The willingness to come ever closer to the core of their being with both celebratory fervor and realistic self-assessment brings them into alignment with their heart's true mission: lasting and luminous self-acceptance.

In the tarot's Major Arcana, Leo's patron saint card is Strength, often depicted by a being clad in glorious white robes approaching a lion's open mouth with open palms. This willingness to come at the world unarmed and heart-first lives at the core of the Leonine call for exposure. Whenever this little love cat has lost its way, the secret is always to summon a palms-up approach rather than a Napoleonic pretentious defense. Showing up in white softness to face life's most seemingly ferocious beasts is this sign's greatest act of courage.

Swapping "I'll show you mine if you show me yours" for simply letting it show, Leo's "me-first" attitude can be channeled into a willingness to "go first" no matter what. Here to teach the rest of the world that dropping our armor is not only possible but highly desirable, these acts of disarmament bring Leos deeper into the dance of core self. Valuing their own humanness allows them to extend this generous acceptance to every person they meet.

Considering their carnivorous nature (alongside the Scorpion, the Lion is the only other explicit meat lover in the zodiac), this willingness to soften may seem paradoxical. Yet Leonine landscapes contain both the jungle cat and the well-tended house pet, reminding us of the sign's capacity for fancy-feasting on all flavors of ferociousness. Even huntresses can consider the humanness of their prey, giving thanks to the succulence of the treats they consume and licking their chops with satisfied satiation. And when Leos choose the path of more fluff and less exhausting force, literally letting the muscles of their mojo relax, they can forge entirely new concepts of success. When these love cats gain confidence in a lifelong capacity to catch their next meal, sweaty moves to stay "on top" need never be the endgame.

Realness

Softening into the sunbaked range of their selfhoods brings Leos into communion with a sparkling destiny forged through relentless realness. Following the lead of their compulsive drives to be exactly as they are at all times, Leos are perpetually brought back to the heart of their own circumstance, compelled to check in with their own personal beats at every turn.

And while what is "real" for them is certainly subject to evolutionary appetite change, there's a remarkable constancy to the Leonine lifetime. You can almost always spot a Leo, whether it's thanks to their stylistic flair, the swagger of their strut (which definitely deserves a theme song), or the feeling that you would still be able to see them even in a darkened room. No matter the situation, Leos seem to carry a signature scent. When the world turns cold or they feel like they've lost their way, returning to this essence is essential, no matter how small the gemstone glint of this proprietary pulsation.

While "cardinal" signs initiate the start of each season (Aries, Cancer, Libra, Capricorn) and "mutable" signs slip-slide us into the next (Sagittarius, Pisces, Gemini, Virgo), "fixed" signs (Leo, Scorpio, Aquarius, Taurus) hunker us down into the center of the Tootsie Pop and work with the solid fullness of willpower, stability, and desire. The "eternal flame" of the three fire signs, Leos must follow what truly lights them up, relentlessly pursuing their heat sources regardless of how they are perceived.

The Queens of un-guilty pleasures and full-bodied passions, Leos are tasked with igniting their entire beings with an all-or-nothingness-fueled appetite. Living, breathing proof that the heart wants what it wants, the Leonine lifetime is best lived from the center of the chest rather than the neck up. Not one for half measures, these bright beings are here to let their realness spill up and over the sides of their cups, learning to banish the shame around "too muchness" and to quite simply bring it on.

Specialness

While this persistent focus on their own interests can sometimes morph into blind self-obsession, at its core it is connected to the kitten's mission to celebrate how special it is at all costs.

As the fifth sign of the zodiac, a number associated with the magic and majesty of laying claim to what we've learned through experience, Leos take the first steps towards truly considering their tastes. Leo marks the moment in our soul's development when we leave the safety of our private lair and step out into the world. After the highly personal journeys of Aries, Taurus, Gemini, and Cancer before it, Leos are built to let their brushes with others refine what they consider beloved. Think of the Leonine lifestyle as a kind of teenage locker left open, papered with band pullout pages and little vanity altars to treasured moments.

The question of their specific incarnation and its contours is perpetually on their hot pink lips, demanding constant attention and incantations that bring it into being. Learning to believe that the world can savor their distinctive flavor with no effort is the kitten's growing edge. When out of alignment, this little fluffball can puff and plump aimlessly, grasping at their bigness as a cover for lurking feelings of less-than-lusciousness.

More than any other sign, Leos are driven by a sense of personal destiny, convinced that they have graced the earth for a carefully chosen purpose ordained by the heavens. And they are absolutely right. Their sparkle and shine is unparalleled in the zodiac, and good goddess do we need their glow. But at the heart of the matter (where a Leo always longs to live), this meet-and-greet with destiny must be a midnight chat between Leo and whatever they deem their god to be. Always checking first with their internal heat source is the key to creating sustainable fire. And when synched up seamlessly with their special flairs, Leos learn that they don't have to break a sweat to become irreplaceable. They simply have to *be*.

Creation

Whether or not they're actual artists or performers, all Leos are here to work with the process of creation, learning to understand the specific sparkle that animates their DNA. Often pigeonholed as the zodiac's crowd-pleasing, jazz-hands performers, Leos actually undergo very subtle processes of show-and-tell. Regardless of whether or not the seats are filled, Leonine acts of creation must first and foremost bear witness to the self. After the watery inner world of Cancer, the sign that directly precedes it, Leo is here to give birth to these private fantasies. These creative acts are akin to a second heart that lives outside the body, and Leos must match the blood type of this second heart in order to thrive.

Indeed, their entire lives must consist of creative acts, and Leo returns us to the original dictionary meaning of the word romance: "a quality or feeling of mystery, excitement, and remoteness from everyday life." Extending far beyond simplistic visions of red roses and white weddings, romance is connected to our capacity to inject magic into the mundane. It helps us remember that our existence alone is worthy of epic mythology. The notorious Leonine capacity for "drama" is actually connected to this magical mission, and Leos are here to remind the rest of us that our existence is worthy of epic mythology. A life worth living is worth living larger, whether that means strutting down the street to an imaginary soundtrack or hair-spraying their notorious manes to high heaven.

At its highest octave of expression, this pleasure-soaked, color-saturated vision can inspire Leo's traveling companions to sparkle and glow alongside the kitten, which in turn can help Leo find the courage to simply sit back and enjoy. Passion must go hand in hand with compassion, which literally means "to feel with." Uncovering the poetry in every gesture and the star-studded quality of every sensation leads Leos closer to both their own hearts and the humanity of others. Leo thus provides a soul train of dancers to help keep the beat for whatever other style is shimmying its way through the center of the crowd.

Leo's curvaceous sign symbol is part lion's mane, part playground equipment, and urges those born of the kitten to dive heart-first into its ice cream swirl, arms up and completely alive to the present. For Leos, play must become a form of prayer. Strategy is swapped for a full-throttle trust in the aliveness that courses through our veins. Stripped down to its barest skin, the Leonine lifetime keeps rhythm with a deceptively simple heartbeat: the cosmic call to become more and more of the selves we long to be and already are. Leos must sport their truest colors, no matter the cost.

This journey into the leopard-print luminosity of Leo's lair is set to a mash-up of Céline Dion's "My Heart Will Go On" and Madonna's "Express Yourself." It is clad in gold lamé, hot pink, and whatever saturated, signature shades your soul wants to sport. It also comes served with plenty of succulent snackables: think mangoes on sticks, over-ripe juicy tomatoes, and bubblegum bubbles ready to burst. Truth be told, Leo is bombastically emboldened and gaudily gorgeous in its unapologetic urge to just be.

So strap on your roller skates, slather yourself in suntan oil, and get ready to shake it to your own bedazzled beat.

LEO

as a Child

magine an endlessly idle summer afternoon, complete with the heady scent of honeysuckle, poolside cheese curls, ice cream truck soundtracks, and absolutely nowhere to go and nothing to do but be, be, be.

The perfectly plumped orb of the orange creamsicle sun, Leonine energy embodies the very essence of childhood, exuding the sheer excitement and unstoppable animation of our original life force. Leo is here to celebrate vitality and remind us that our mere existence is always more than enough reason to walk this earth with majesty. In childhood, we all catch a glimpse of what it means to carry this credo. For Leos, the trick is to never stop courting this mistress of miniature-me magic.

For Leo children, this life is a delectable treasure to behold and adore. They clutch it close to their hot little hearts, tucked in and tender. Filled with the pulse-quickening spirit of unquenchable hope, life arrives in their upturned palms like a birthday present, complete with shiny ribbons and glittery wrapping paper. During the perpetual process of self-exploration, Leo children learn how to harness the power of the personal, how to lay claim to their turf, and how to inject their strongest rainbow-sherbet-saturated sensations into even the most mundane of life's moments.

THE PATRON SAINT OF PLAY

Whatever the age of the Leo, the sign itself is the patron saint of childhood, and this patronage is deeply connected to acts of play and creation. The Leo child is the embodiment of the verb "to play," and is most fully themselves when deep in the flow of gushing expression and unstructured freedom. Quite simply, Leo youth just wanna have fun. And they are undeniable proof that play is the worthiest of all art forms.

Take a moment to consider the onomatopoeic sound of the word "Leo." Just three letters and ending in a vowel ready to embark on a Mediterranean holiday, Leo is the simplest sound in the zodiac. It's a straightforward sparkle that feels as luscious to roll in the mouth as a hard candy with a liquid center. In childhood, Leos must harness this open-endedness and stripped-down sense of self. Over time, they learn how to constantly recreate themselves through acts of make-believe. Every moment becomes proof of their own deep magic. When they embrace the magic of each moment, no matter how minuscule, they remember to treat life like a grand inheritance they've been gifted.

The act of play invites us to fearlessly bring forth our own whimsical inner landscapes. It's a reverential ode to the sheer joy of being alive. This act is successful not because it's recognized by others or because it results in some tangible reward. Rather, the reward is the process of becoming more and more ourselves. To play is to put strategy aside. To relax our defenses. To believe that life wants to lift us and catch us and swing us up and over the bar. To remember that we are not an accident. To understand that life is here and waiting for us to enter it. And for Leo children, everything must conspire to support this belief.

Although play doesn't need to bear any tangible results, as they engage in these guileless acts of joy, Leo children inevitably develop some attachment to seeing how they affect the world that surrounds them. The key is to encourage play while also making sure they don't become overly dominant in their surroundings. The results of play should always be pure, with greater emphasis placed on the "being" rather than the "doing." At whatever stage of development these young cats find themselves in, they must surrender to the moment of creation, when the maker lets go of what gets made. Whether it's as low-stakes as a backyard mud pie or as intense as their first serious homework assignment, Leo children thrive when they are focused on the motions of the action itself rather than the action's results.

Yet these acts of creation must always bear the signature of the self. When the process is deeply aligned with what the Leo child hopes to create in the first place, there is seamlessness in the sparkle. But when they inevitably run into external rules and authorities, these little love cats simply must find ways of adding their own bit of flavor and flair, no matter the limitations. As they enter adolescence, finding their flair becomes even more vital. Perhaps more than any other teen sign, they need to seek out new ways of letting their creativity shine. Whether it's bumper-sticker proclamations on their rides or signature streaks of pink through their hair, Leos are built to leave a glitter trail through the high school hallways. Even if it's simply penning a heart-shaped dot above the decimal mark in an all-too-linear math equation, making their pizazz known is critical to their development.

CINEMATIC CHORE LISTS

The fire function is forever larger-than-life, and this plumping-up process begins early on for Leos, who may feel actively oppressed by the limits of the mundane world almost from the moment they arrive. And while some Leo children might follow the rules if they get to be the leader, in their hearts they often seek escape in a more exotic realm.

Preparing a young Leo for a lifetime of colliding with the mundanity of existence means making sure they are equipped with the most vibrant color palette possible. If they're engaged in chores that feel oppressive, they might need to find a way to transcend this experience. Imagining that they're playing a starring role in a show called "Life," which occasionally requires them to make the bed or wash the dishes, can help these love cats find the epic in the everyday. Such a skill set will be useful well into adulthood, when everyday drudgery can often feel endless and inescapable.

Leonine children can sometimes have a startling sense of immediacy about them. They may appear constantly on the edge of the next big feeling, ready to burst into tears, rage, or a song and dance. At the core of these cravings is the desire to be adored. To be held by this world in constant awe. Even the most introverted of Leos craves this kind of glory, and if they're not tap-dancing and tugging on your wrist to get you to watch, they will still harbor secret longings to be looked at in some fashion.

Indeed, at this most tender of times, teaching the Leo babe how to grapple with the full range of their feelings is critical, as they tend to ride the roller coaster of extremely high highs followed by bottomed-out lows, especially as they enter their teen years. Chasing the intensity of "solar" hits starts to pattern itself in their youth, as Leo kiddies hungrily seek out dramatic moments of self-mythology and expression. Learning to navigate these slopes starts by fully supporting their most heat-saturated pink and turquoise sensations. As they weather their own emotional intensity, they build faith in the belief that these colors are part of their very soul's palette, available at any moment.

Telling a Leo child they're "feeling too much" or to "stop that crying" signals a kind of soul death that will echo throughout the rest of their days. Allowing young Leos to emote the rainbow without reprimand affirms their fundamental right to spill over the edges and beyond the lines. Additionally, young Leos should be gently encouraged to spend quiet time amidst their feelings. This will help them learn to live with the fluctuations without immediately demanding a reaction. Channeling feelings into finger paint, choreographing a private dance number in the basement, or strutting down the neighborhood block can replenish and restore a young Leo's soul, providing proof of their Technicolor while teaching them how to cope with and celebrate every shade of emotion, all on their own.

RULERS OF THE CASTLE

Whether they're doling out dolls to the neighborhood kids, deciding who will play with which one and creating backstories for each Barbie, or staking out a certain area of the house as their own little kingdom, Leo youths are always looking to assert their right to inhabit their own lair.

With a reputation for sometimes taking on the role of a dictator, it's important that their parents and mentors help guide these urges for rulership early on, to ensure that the young Leo leads with love rather than force. When they feel secure in their own signature flair, there is no child in the zodiac more generous with their heart space. It's most often the Leo child who's willing to extend a bejeweled hand to lift others up onto the top of the fort for heaps of fierce fun.

Leo children are best supported when they're given the right to enact self-dominion, even when it comes to mundane situations. If you bear a Leo babe, letting them exercise their personal appetites grants them an everlasting key to their castles, whether it's picking out their lunchbox snacks or the outfit they'll wear to a family function. To be seen and felt is of the highest importance, complete with signature color palettes. In fact, playing dress-up can be a prime arena for self-exploration and self-determination, and Leo children truly flourish when diving into a closet of fantasy frocks. Whether they choose glittering gemstones, a spandex superhero suit, or simply a piece from their parent's work ensemble, the act of slipping in and out of threads is a powerful part of their process of self-empowerment.

Whether or not the Leonine youth is a born performer doesn't matter. Any chance to experience the self's reflection and be "received" is highly desired. Whether it's locked in the closet recording a personal podcast or watching footage of themselves dancing in the backyard, the process of solitary mirroring is a critical one for Leo children. Even before their gifts go out into the world for feedback from humanity, these early, more private exchanges help Leos build an unshakable trust in their own identities that can stave off feelings of not-enoughness that might come later. Filling their own cups with the strength and security of their self-expression at a young age will ensure that the little love cats are able to lick their own wounds and celebrate their own victories.

SENSITIVE STUFFED ANIMAL PILEUPS

Playfully reflective self-awareness and megawatt feelings are part and parcel of the little Leo's deep desire to get closer to this world. Like the love cats they are, Leo children want to rub up on the furniture and leave their scents. They want to make sure they are *felt* by everything that surrounds them. While Earth signs (Taurus, Virgo, and Capricorn) are known for their deep sensuality, Leo youths also love to touch and be touched. If conditions are right and they feel supported, they can be some of the most affectionate youths on the astro block, clutching whatever they love close to their hearts. As they pet their fuzzy stickers, comb glossy purple pony hair, dive into plush pink stuffed animal pileups, or emblazon their bestie's neck with a golden "Forever Friends" heart, Leo children are constantly attempting to close the gap between themselves and what they care about most.

This desire for closeness and magical mirroring means that Leonine youths often have a rather animistic view of their surroundings. They can be passionate about their most beloved toys, often naming them and giving them full life histories that include birth certificates. A Leo child might even go as far as to worry about a lone piece of pasta in the trash that has no traveling companion. This process of injecting the material world with narrative should be lifted up and celebrated in the young Leo and never deemed silly. Leonine hearts are pumping outside their bodies after all. If encouraged, this youthful tendency towards animism can strengthen the generosity of their spirits.

In Carl Jung's (who also happened to be born under the sign of the love cat) primary psychological functions, fire energy is connected to the intuitive function. At its core, this function is proof of our capacity to believe in the beauty of our own existence. The belief that we mean something and that we can sense, in our wildest moments of freedom and flow, a larger connection to all that exists. That we are not separate from this world. For Leo children, this connection is vibrant and alive. Every object that they see, whether it's a blade of grass or a plastic Barbie slipper, reflects themselves and their self-expressive stories.

2

LEO
as an Adult

As young Leos prepare to leave the plush pink of their bouncy castles for the harshness of the wider world, the transition into adulthood can be a startling one. Playground power struggles lead to higher-stakes encounters with authority later on, and the key to a full adulthood lies in stoking and tending the eternal flame.

With time, the gap between the jungle cat and house cat identities can widen, and Leos may find themselves swinging wildly between voracious, leopard-spotted grasps at power and prowess and rhinestone-collar retreats into the kitty cup for petting and grooming. Growing up seems to necessitate ferocity first, and the inner softness and tenderness of the fluffball can start to wither.

The answer lies, as with all things Leonine, in a simple but potent act. As the Leo ages, the call home to their central mission gets more and more vital: to live heart-first. In fact, more than any other sign, Leonine beings are asked to "grow down" as they age. This means they must remember their core selves at every turn.

THE 20S: HUNGRY, HUNGRY KITTENS

As young Leos first head out into the world, their central focus is often on maintaining the sense of "specialness" they developed as children. Their experiences as young adults can be direct reflections of how much or how little they were adored and affirmed.

In either case, the usual romantic fervor of any sign's early 20s is amplified a thousand-fold in Leos, and they come at the world hungry for vittles to boost their vitality. These ravenous youths can often find themselves in the throes of dramatic obsessions, sometimes shifting their notorious forces to another being or beings that they believe necessary to confirming and stoking their flames. And as they enter into their first serious partnerships and begin to let the world's limitations in, a harsh skin sometimes starts to form over their soft hearts, which plump and puff in reaction to all this new criticism.

Astrologically, this time is all leading the Leos towards their "Saturn Return," a cosmic comeuppance that occurs around the ages of 28–29. Connected to the earthy pragmatism of the sign of Capricorn, this period can feel like a

LEO

reality check for Leos in particular, as their sunbaked tropical island light starts to look more like the harsh exposure of the morning after. The lifelong question of how to collaborate with the contours of life as it is gets activated, and the young Leo is asked to envision this time as a kind of spiritual haiku. They must learn to dance in whatever room is available, no matter the size, and paint with whatever colors are currently on hand.

Gifted with extremely potent life forces, the question of which way to point their love beams is always of the highest importance. And as the late 20s crest, Leos start to become aware of their true prowess on a durational level. They come to understand that the promise of their specialness is here to incarnate on the earthly plane rather than to just be chased into the clouds for its addictive highs.

THE 30S: TASTE THE RAINBOW

Following the Saturn Return, a core piece of the Leo's being has been recovered, and there can be a sweet feeling of getting scooped out and washed clean. Leos find themselves all the way back on the shores of a more settled sense of self, and this can never be taken away. As Leos enter their 30s, they start to stand proudly and firmly at the center of their bouncy castles and catch glimpses of a glittery mission that is truly meant to warm the world.

During this decade, Leos first start to come into communion with the concept of channeling. Creative actions come through them, and they don't have to push so hard on the pedal of proving. As they start to release into relishing passion projects, guided by instinct and intuition, they can begin to creatively marinate projects and partnerships. They can now also trust that their essence will flavor whatever gets tossed into the frying pan without having to make sure that their names are explicitly listed on the menu.

Towards the end of this decade, the Leo gets their first hit of the "Pluto Square" astrological aspect, and this underground planet can take the burgeoning fluffball straight into the belly of its beasties. For Leos, this means starting to truly explore questions of power, success, and sustainable strength, and to consider swapping gold stars and carefully autographed names for a curiosity about the star-studded stuff they contain. During this time, the young Leo starts to explore how to "stay with" every feeling that arises, rather than instantaneously translating everything into larger-than-life emotions that must be immediately strung up in neon lights.

Pluto is also the planet of deep feeling integration. It takes us to the bottom of our wells and the undersides of our logs in order to examine all of our creepy crawly impulses. A successful mission to the underworld is evidenced by our capacity to feel rather than our ability to fix. The unstoppable glow of Leo's headlamp can help reveal this. This is a time for Leos to start probing exactly what they are made of and to consider the snackability of all their shades, rather than favoring only the ripest tomatoes and summer fruits.

THE 40S: SPARKLE AND SHINE SYMPHONY

The dawn of the 40s can signal a period of tumult for the glamour pusses, as they begin to sense the physical limitations of the bodies they inhabit. No matter where they sit on the spectrum of vanity, Leos will start to come up against the gnawing sense that they won't be the first souls to live forever in the fullest glory of their Texan-sized manes.

But rather than a plastic-surgery-fueled frenzy to hungrily grasp at forever young, this decade offers Leos the chance to revise their beauty standards and learn to truly "behold" themselves as their bodies shift and change. The 40s love cat is invited to celebrate whichever aspects of their physical selves feel most on fire. And this can become a quietly insular, self-seductive process, with the 40s Leo staying home at night for epic sessions of self-massage.

This decade is about understanding appetites and desires. In their 40s, Leos are called to carefully consider the menu options. They become choosier in their selections of partners and projects. Rather than simply stalking prey out of animalistic instinct, 40s Leos learn to banish this scarcity mentality and to trust that, if they pass on a certain snack, there will certainly be more soul food on the way.

Astrologically, this era is dominated by the "Uranus Opposition," a planetary transit that wakes us up and shakes us up (commonly part of the notorious "midlife crisis). This planetary shock jock invites Leo to integrate its opposite sign of Aquarius, the cosmic queen of panned-out perspectives and collective consciousness. While Leos start to get hits of creative "channeling" in their 30s, the 40s Leo begins to deeply grasp what it means to "play their part" in a complex symphony. They become more concerned with collaborative efforts rather than merely waiting for their next solo. If they can rise to the occasion, the Leos in their late 40s learn about their vital connections to the whole. By doing less and being more, their presences alone can become some of the most powerful creative forces imaginable.

THE 50S: LIFE IN THE SHADE

Armed with a newfound concept of sustainable glamour and a growing trust in the vital role of their symphonic instruments, Leos enter the 50s with a nocturnal trail of glitter in their wake. The thought of going "softly" actually starts to bring out even more of their notorious sparkle, and it is here that Leos begin to learn to truly integrate their call towards tenderness. They recover that original "Strength" tarot card mission of disarming themselves and coming at the world palms-up.

Astrologically, this era is dominated by the "Chiron Return," an event that calls for deep sensitivity and a willingness to access our feelings no matter how much it hurts. Minor planet Chiron is the zodiac's softest spot, a little package we've arrived with that may not even be ours to carry. This archetype is the gateway to our humanness, a reminder that not everything has to be fixed to be felt. And for the Leonine pride, this can be a tall order.

Trusting in this process of self-tenderizing is Leo's deepest work during the 50s, and the love cats are called to truly consider what an internal experience looks like. They come up against their factory settings of a life forever lived in the full light of day. Yet there are untold treasures tucked into these shadowy places, and the maturing Leo is asked to get a little loony with it all. At this time, they may find creative inspiration in the midnight hours as they craft their own particular brand of silk-robed sensuality. They're invited to come into communion with these glamourous ghosties rather than trying to push away any darkness that arises.

THE 60S: THE INNER THRONE

As the 50s close, Leos come into their second Saturn Return, which beckons them into a brand of boldness that will shine bright for the rest of their days. This is the time of deepest "earth" element integration for the sign, and the call is to develop a profound trust in their inner authority. They have the chance to step out into this decade clad in precious metals and soul alignment.

"Who's really calling the shots?" asks the 60s Leo. "And what does a life well lived truly look like for me?" As they begin to walk the rooms of their castle at this juncture in life, the answers they find may surprise them. Initially, this can lead to scrambled attempts to rectify anything that doesn't seem to be in soul-shaped order. Another common feeling is a profound sadness over what's been "wasted." On the surface, the early part of this decade may appear to bring on the blues, especially as the Leo reflects on the accolades and achievements they have earned in life. While these may have provided initial satisfaction, it's possible they haven't proven to be sustainable sources of sparkle and glow.

Yet this is all part of the rainbow integration of feelings for the later-in-life Leo. It's designed to push them towards that internal source of heat and power that can never be tamped down. Before they hurtle towards the psychiatrist in search of prescriptions to shut off the sadness valves, they're called to sit steadily with these feelings, to integrate them, and to let them lead to an assessment of their truest sources of pride.

What have they created that they'd be willing to risk their bodies for in a house fire? In the long process of "growing back down" to meet their original sources of ignition, the 60s signal a decade of pageantry and regality. In the hopes of creating a legacy that's built to last, the 60s Leo seeks only the most sustainable sources of diamonds to mine.

THE 70S+: RETURN TO SOURCE

Following the emotional diamond-mining and throne-claiming of the 60s, the 70s arrive as a breath of candy-coated air. The original package of presence Leos were handed as youths is promptly regifted to them. This mature Leo has the deepest capacity to harness the heat that originally ignited their birth. The Leonine generosity of spirit starts to spill over during this decade as the little love cat settles in, gives it up, and turns it loose to a higher law.

This is the moment when the abundant sense of sparkly treasure really flowers, and these felines come into their own as cosmic coaches and cheerleaders for all those mere mortals who surround them. Genius guidance counselors and emboldened blood transfusers for whatever has gotten stale and sepia-toned, these wise Leos are all spryness and sparkle, lit up as though from the great beyond. The keyword during this decade is "bask," and it's here that Leos learn to lie down in whatever sunlit patch is close by, full up with the feeling that they've got nothing to lose and everything to give.

Astrologically, if the Leo makes it into the 80s (and they often do, for no other sign loves the sheer exuberance of existence quite like this sign), they hit their "Uranus Return," a cosmic transit that electrifies the relationship between their personal identity and collective gifts. While the energy builds towards this moment, whatever simply succulent, straightforward sensation first opened their hearts as youths must be uncovered and recovered. As their whole lives flash dance before their wide eyes, these wise kittens see, suddenly, that it was all for the love of it, whatever it was. And it was never in vain.

LEO

as a Parent

As the zodiac's divine diva creators, there can be no act more elevated in the Leo's eyes than bequeathing their mini me's to the parched earth—precious packages meant to be extensions of momma's or poppa's magic mission. The creative process of birthing and shaping a wee soul can truly be one of Leo's greatest artistic endeavors. And, if they're lucky, the children of Leos will get to bask in the heat of a loyal love that opens them up to their highest potential as distinctive beings, forever lit by their lustrous lineage.

The most elevated form of parenting rests in the Leo parent's capacity for understanding the boundaries between themselves and their little ones. Leo parents must support the distinctive passions and projects of their children rather than projecting their own proprietary personhood onto impressionable youth. For the child of Leo progenitors, there can sometimes be a struggle to understand where their parents end and they begin. Whether the Leo parent is mirroring their moves in the front row of a jazz dance performance or carefully arranging hair clippings from their offspring in a beloved scrapbook, their children may start to suspect that the glorious sense of Leonine selfhood trumps their own specificity.

But if Leo parents can remember that the child they've created is more than a mere art object, the generosity they can show this second spirit is immeasurable, and raising children can connect both parties to their most beloved solar-powered sources for the rest of their shared lives.

PREGNANCY PILLOW PLUMPS: PREPPING FOR ARRIVAL

For the Leo who is giving birth, pregnancy itself can become an impassioned obsession, and the plumped-up Leo is often given over to stopping strangers on the street to discuss every nuance of their changing bodies, practically convincing themselves that they're the first animal in the kingdom to spring something from their loins. Because of Leo's complex relationship with their physical container, this can be a good time to allow the love cat to glamorize and dramatize their process, morning sickness and all. For the Leo who wants to believe that their gorgeousness is perpetually unshakable, spa days, cosmetic treats, and naked pregnancy pics can help bolster this new parent's solid sense of self as their body evolves.

And as they grow this little one inside them or prepare for its arrival through other means, Leo parents are urged to pay special attention to their roles in crafting a narrative for a being they've not yet met. Choosing names, color palettes, and tiny ensembles can lead these Leos into a frenzy. They begin to project mythologies onto their minis before the child's cells have evolved beyond the size of a cherry pit. While crafting a complete life story for little Enid or Edgar can be a playful act of passion for the Leo parent, waiting to actually give birth before names are chosen is one way to forge a more realistic connection with their soon-to-be child. This helps ensure that the kiddie gets a say, becoming a star in their own right rather than a mere player under the Leo parent's directorial gaze.

More than any other sign, the perceived loss of some of their youthful distinction can fill Leos with postpartum sadness. In preparation for their offspring's arrival, Leo parents-to-be are invited to engage more deeply in personal passions, such as keeping a scheduled "friends' night out" or preserving a beloved pottery class. No matter how the Leo is choosing to become a parent, bringing pageantry to this pre-arrival process is key to maintaining both a sense of self and an open space for the new child to inhabit.

FREE TO BE: PARENTING YOUNG CHILDREN

The early years of a Leo's parenting process can seem paradoxical. The Glitter Kitten searches to balance the popsicle-stick pleasures of playground antics that they've always loved with a deepening sense of dependence on their little one. Their personal passions for playing make-believe and dress-up commingle with fears that their own sense of specialness may be getting absorbed into their bundle of joy.

At this stage, it is critical for the Leo parent to both maintain their own personal agenda, saving ample time for the activities that brought them alive before their little one arrived, and continuously check in about the specifics of their offspring. Ensuring that the story of their babe is auto-biographical rather than biographical—penned by this new tiny person instead of ghostwritten by momma or poppa—can become a Leonine parental fine art.

The theme of competition can rear its head here both between parent and child, and between their child and the world. Whether in the form of zealous praise of their youngster's specific hopes and dreams or directly pitting their little one against their fellow playmates, the Leo parent's heroic narratives for their minis can take on mythic proportions. Overscheduled offspring of Leo parents may start to build serious resentment. They may feel like they're tiny, imprisoned gymnasts whose bodies are literally getting shaped against their will by the Olympic-level parenting of the unaware Leo. In turn, great care must be taken at this juncture to truly listen and learn from their child's cues. They must inquire deeply about desired hobbies and personal passions.

Rather than helicopters, Leo parents often take on the role of luxury private jets, either deeply engaged in the lives of their little ones without truly respecting their ground-level specificity, or disappearing into their own glamourama zones of creation while completely ignoring the needs of their progeny passengers. In extreme cases, their children can become precious jeweled accessories that either match their outfits or are put back in the box. This relegates the children to auxiliary aesthetics rather than flesh-and-blood souls.

When in doubt, returning to the exuberant immediacy of play is always the sweetest medicine for Leo parents of young children. Their love of over-the-top mania can be channeled into the sheer delight of their little one at this stage. Leo parents are ready to fully immerse themselves in the fantastical worlds of their fresh little friends. It is natural for them to take an immersive method-acting approach and inhabit imaginary roles, the goal being to transform the lives of their littles into all-access amusement parks of overstuffed animals. Finding balance rests in constantly checking to ensure that their babe is still loving the ride.

HIGH SCHOOL SUPERLATIVES: TEEN PARENTING

Whatever the experience of their own adolescence, the Leo parent has a penchant for powerfully projecting mythologies onto their young adult. They often wind up deciding their teen's high school superlatives before they have even set foot in the school halls. Taken too far, the Leo parent may look to live out some of their unlived cat lives through their young kitten, attempting to mold their youth into the jock, science whizz, or badass beauty-behind-the-bleachers they never were.

Remaining fully attentive to their child's burgeoning personhood is hypercritical at this stage. And grounding themselves in the here and now of their teen's experience through current cultural tastes can help them connect with their child, glamorously and gleefully. Whether it's a beloved playlist, a new crush, or the latest-trending look, the Leo parent is encouraged to ask questions and listen to their teen without judgment. They should imagine that their adolescent is a fascinating new friend instead of a teen dream mirror.

However, this friend status must be carefully negotiated, as Leo parents can become the zodiac's DILFs and MILFs with a casual toss of their manes. Perhaps more so than any other sign on the astrological block, Leos can be tantalized by the possibility of a second adolescence. While

Leo parents should definitely draw inspiration from the latest sounds and styles as refracted through their children, they're encouraged to craft their own custom blends. They need to be careful not to co-opt their kid's appetites or blur the delicate sexual and emotional lines by too much fraternizing with their child's friends.

At the stage when their child starts to blossom into a fully separate person, deciding their particular brand of authority is vital. The Leo parent can sometimes oscillate between the distant dictator who pulls up the drawbridges and locks their loved ones inside and the desperate bestie who attempts to remain "cool" by throwing the doors wide open and confusing the parental role.

Allowing their child both freedom and fortifications is a delicate balance for the Leo parent, who wants to impose their will while remaining eternally beloved in the eyes of their child. Negotiating these lines with greater ease lies in applying the Leo's characteristically open-hearted curiosity to their teen's hopes and dreams. Leos should seek to understand the intricacies of the being underneath their roof and shape curfew times accordingly.

THE GOLDEN LION YEARS: GROWING INTO ADULTHOOD

As Leo's offspring leaves the lair, there can be a precious clinging to what once was. The children of an aging Leo parent often find themselves subject to gifts made from repurposed memories. They may receive little pillows fashioned from childhood blankets. Baby booties can show up in their mailboxes at unexpected moments. During this phase, the Leo parent is called to celebrate the storyline they share with their child. They must continue to pay close attention to the adult person their child is becoming, being careful not to project the treasured past onto their freshly minted adult.

The notorious Leonine need to feel the glowing giveback of the love they give out is often amplified during this time. The certitude of a shared habitat makes way for the shakier ground of separate residences and separate lives. The perpetually childlike Leonine qualities can be magnified here, and the aging parent's voracious hunger for love can grow in proportion to distance. Leo parents may consistently ask whether their child still treasures or needs them. The grown child of a Leo parent may find themselves having to parent the people who raised them, as wide-eyed, tender-hearted Mom or Dad blows up their phone with petulant tantrums and deep yearnings.

For the aging Leo parent, pride levels can also start to increase. These Leos are in the process of steeling themselves against their own decreased mobilities and a sense of separateness from their children. Rather than tending to their needs in a straightforward way, Leo parents may ignore their hurts or nurse them silently. In these cases, it is best for them to be as transparent as possible so that real healing can take place. Yet this is also the time when a deep spiritual and artistic renaissance is available to the mature Leo parent. Finding themselves back in the arms of more personal passions can offer sweet relief and rekindle their individual sparkles. Learning to truly live and let live as an adult, Leo parents return both parties to their most majestic senses of self.

ELEMENTAL PARENTING

Whether you're the offspring of a Leo who's looking for guidance on how to better connect or a Leonine parent searching for the best approach to rearing your little one's sign, use the elemental guide below to make the most of your lineage.

Fellow Fire Signs (Aries, Leo, Sagittarius): Energies at home are big and bold for these BBQ babes and their parents, and splashy shouting and oversized feelings lend the household a hot and heavy flair. The key here is to allow each other a full range for self-expression. Remain extra sensitive to individual distinctions. This may mean quite literally identifying specific domains for each person to inhabit, with playrooms and art studios clearly mapped out (no matter how small the living quarters). Bedroom dance parties (and later, wedding dance floors) can be the perfect way to start celebrating one another, with the parent and child taking turns being the DJ and the star performer.

Water Signs (Cancer, Scorpio, Pisces): For these deep-feeling, intensely private water babes, a Leo parent can sometimes seem startlingly obvious in their emotions, and parents are advised to allow their little mer-person plenty of alone time without trying to pry open their secret diaries. Both of these astro energies are strong feelers, the difference resting in the internal, terrarium-like sensations of the water babe and the more externalized trumpet tantrums of the Leo. As they both age, a shared penchant for the past can polarize into hard-lined fighting to control the family narrative. Celebrate memories together with slideshows and scrapbooks rather than I said/you said battles to rewrite ancient history.

Air Signs (Libra, Aquarius, Gemini): The easy-breezy intellectual energy of air can feel like a place of deep fear for the highly personal, heavily attached Leo. Leo parents may try to coax and conjure big reactions from their air-sign offspring, convinced that their kiddie's lack of tears or screams of joy are signs that they're not fully engaged in the act of living. When flipped, the air-sign child can struggle to understand what all this drama is about, and they're invited to let their Leo parent ride out their highs and lows without trying to explain it all away. Both of these astro energies can be idealistically expressive. Shared creative projects, such as family vacation planning, help them realize their visions together.

Earth Signs (Capricorn, Taurus, Virgo): For heavily earthbound children, the cinematically enhanced world of the Leonine parent can sometimes feel like a superficial landscape of imaginary, ego-driven antics. And for the Leo parent, the key lies in letting their little one explore the physical world without demanding that they fly away into fantasy. They must be content in letting their offspring discover creative means of repurposing what's right here, right now. Together, themes of structure and authority are amplified. As they learn to live together, they're both called to soften entrenched positions and stuck viewpoints. Simple activities like potluck cooking can help them respect each other's desires and celebrate the distinctive flavors they have to offer.

4

LEO
in Love

While Taurus and Libra may be the signs ruled by rose-petal planet Venus, Leo has the cosmic corner on lavish love, which is lit by the eternal flame pulsations of the midday sun. The lust of Leos is quite literal, and they were born to live it (with just one more letter, Leo becomes the word Love). The zodiac's everlasting romantics in the classical definition of the word, these fancy felines are perpetually poised for mutual adoration fests and heavy petting, letting lovers lap them up like sweet cream. They carry their paramours across their big cat backs with unwavering passion.

The growing edge for these little love kittens lies in learning to receive. They must open their arms to their lovers as separate beings and magnetize what they desire with sweet allurement rather than blind dominance. Hyped up on their own heat, Leos can sometimes plan the whole Hawaiian vacation before checking in with their traveling companions about their choice of luxurious locale. But when Leos learn to disco dance in time with a true give-and-take, they liberate even more of their precious hearts.

This can turn them into hot tubs full of healing waters, ripe and ready for anyone who wants to take a dip.

TELL IT TO MY HEART: CRUSHES AND COURTSHIP

As with all flame-on fire signs, Leo comes at love in plain sight. But unlike the sometimes-painful obviousness of phallic Aries or the wildly elusive stylings of fly-by-night Sag, Leo has a profound urge to demonstrate its fancy flair. Thus it can transform the crushing-and-courting process into a chance to exercise its creative muscle.

More than any other sign, there's something of the classic sweetheart in Leo, and at any stage of life, the early throes of a love affair can carry the body spray scent of teenage mall infatuation. The Leo is convinced that they are the first one to ever get all hot and bothered. They feel as though love has never been lived quite like this before. That the pavement underneath their feet is lighting up like a personalized dance floor, or that the birds have broken into pop music ballads composed just for them.

A perpetual prom night of personalized passion,

early-stage Leo loves are injected with melodrama. Even the most minimalistic Lion (if there truly is such a thing) will engage in some pumped-up proportions in the throes of romance. Like a neon Miami Beach night or a high-rolling weekend in Vegas, there is an irrationally over-the-top quality to Leo's infatuations. And whatever the response by their chosen beloved, the love cats can run on the fumes of the love drug like no other sign, full-up on the life blood of a new affair like a romantic tick. And while this quality is part and parcel of the Leonine capacity to love through the apocalypse, gentle reminders that their love drug is brought on by the presence of an actual complex human with a history can help the Leo evolve beyond the next hit of hedonism.

Regardless of the outcome of dating explorations, Leos are encouraged to celebrate their capacity for trust at all costs. This can be tough and tender medicine for little Leo, as the end of affairs can bring them into some of the darkest depths of any sign. Their capacity to hop into the hot tub and start making promises is directly proportionate to the innocence they lose. But to learn to love again anyway, raising their lighters high above the ashes, is exactly why

Leos exist in the first place. Their heartbeat beneath the heartbreak stands as a testament to their strength.

ETERNAL FLAME: THE LONG-TERM LEO LOVER

The Leonine lover is built to last—a solid-gold nugget that nestles into a beloved's arms for the long haul. Regardless of the form durational partnerships take or the gender identification of the little love cat, there is something of the *Brides Magazine* happily-ever-after that shapes their spirits. Even in the unhitched Leo, there's still a flavor of serial monogamy that takes root, transforming even one-night stands into epic poems scratched into bathroom walls in bubble letters.

In long-term affairs, the generous potential of the Leo is magnified, and in these partnerships they evidence their incredible solar-paneled staying powers. "Devotion" is the guiding light for these long-haul Leos, and they can require a bit of upkeep to feel solid on their romantic thrones. Leaving little love notes and packages around the house helps keep Leo's emotional pillows fluffed. And when they feel safely loved-up-on, the Leonine commitment is unparalleled, renewing its wedding vows through daily acts of devotion.

Long-term Leos are urged to come closer to their romantic growing edge: accommodating inevitable carnal change and opening up to separateness. To last through the night, Leos must learn to understand their lovers as evolving planets in their own right rather than solar-powered satellites fueled only by the Leo's core desires. Cultivating the capacity to remain curious is vital, and Leos in long-haul love are urged to present options to their partners rather than signed, sealed, and delivered statements. "I've booked the tickets to Belize, we leave at 7pm" might be swapped for something like: "Right now, all I can think about is us prancing through humid jungles in matching unitards. Is that something you'd be interested in?"

And when they face up to their fears of waning affection and wounded pride, long-term Leo lovers can find the space for self-driven pursuits that keep the internal flame bright. If their partner isn't feeling their particular heat at a given moment, Leos are urged to take "love vacations" by engaging in acts inspired by their affections without having to demand their partner's full-throttle participation. Taking a romantic getaway for one or crafting a letter to their beloved that they simply read to themselves can bring the Leo back into communion with the point of all this sweet ardor: to maintain their lusty life force by filling their own love cup from the inside out.

RIDE OR DIE: LION-SIZED FRIENDSHIPS

The intensity of Leo's romantic love affairs spills over into their more platonic friendships. They are often playful in their pulsations, ready to radiate outwardly and touch everyone who surrounds them with sunshine. Minus Leo's itchier insecurities of amorous adoration, friends of Leo can benefit from the love cat's oversized heart.

Central to these friendships is a sense of soul recognition, and a Leo who feels truly seen and understood in their essence can return the favor times a billion, beaming their love lights onto others in a mutual melt of delicious appreciation. There's a buffet-style quality to these exchanges, as both parties are allowed to bring more and more of themselves to the table. This results in second and third servings of support, with whipped cream on top. And if the Leo has extra cash to spare, they love to fête a friend, planning impromptu shopping sprees and weekends with besties, and going all-out on the bubbly.

Regardless of their level of social-butterfly status, all Leos thrive with a core group of ride-or-dies, and they're usually ready to literally donate their organs to whoever has pledged allegiance. And when they're careful to cultivate qualities of deep listening, paying close attention to the nuances of their friends' narratives, they can tap straight into their pals' bloodstreams. Choosing love over judgment is always the answer, and when they let themselves be fully present with friends rather than preachy, they become champions of virtually any cause they recognize as heart-centric.

Deep Leonine friendships are 'til death do us part, and the greatest triumph of a Leonine life can be the epic party at their funerals, complete with endless toasts to the person they really and truly were. To capitalize on the festivities, a Leo might even stage these kinds of celebrations of self before they actually depart, honoring thresholds in soul development the rest of us might be too shy to feast on.

Whatever the occasion, the Leo comes ready to get down, and the earnest emotion in their party-starting will forever fuel their companionship conga line.

ELEMENTAL EROTICA: SIGN-BY-SIGN COLLISIONS

Astrological pairings go far beyond good/bad binaries, and every cosmic collision has worthy treasures to mine. Check out the below descriptions for quick-and-dirty tips on what kind of lusty learnings the Leo is in for with each of the signs.

ARIES: Fellow fire sign Aries comes on just as fiercely and fully in love as little Leo, with a straightforward sexual focus that fans Leo's desire for tantalizing transparency. Battles for getting "on top" can produce growth when they learn to let each other take turns in the lead. Leo's more leisurely glitter shines when Aries is allowed to handle the heroic logistics. This leaves Leo content to trust in their right to regality. The undying innocence of both signs can blossom together, as their clear carnal commitment reminds them of their shared capacity for trust. Transcending heartbreak and personal history, these two hop back into the ring together, ready to keep it lit through thick and thin.

TAURUS: Both of these signs are of the "fixed" modality, signaling a penchant for rooted entrenchment and profound underground power sources. Taurus flowers open in the wake of Leo's seemingly unending rays, and Leo is magnetized by Taurus' sweet stability. A rock-solid partnership that can veer towards the staid, the gateway to growth comes through body knowledge, as each helps the other to trust their gut. Both signs are scratch 'n' sniff, touchy feelers, and unabashed sensuality is a carnal cause for celebration. From breakfast in bed to elaborately prepared dinner platters to simply rolling in the sheets and rubbing up on each other, it's a beautifully basic, skin-and-bones affair.

GEMINI: These signs can be both circulatory and full of spring, and there's something fresh and ready about their partnership, which perpetually promises the eternal elixir of youth through its rainbow of possibilities. Whether hitting the club or hosting house parties in their lair, these two thrive on colliding with the world at large, relishing each other's emotionally perceptive reads on the souls of those they meet in the streets. For fixed Leo, Gemini's butterfly wings can sometimes spark fears about lack of loyalty. And Leo's unwavering affection can leave the bee searching for a way out of the cloying honey. But with open telephone lines of communication, these two proverbial teenagers can always talk it out, reigniting their passion through carefully penned love letters and shared secrets.

CANCER: On the surface, Cancer's internal waters and Leo's externalized flame don't appear to mix and mingle, but together, this can be a deliciously loony, midnight-skinny-dipping trip into the pools of personal passion. Cancer's wild inner world finds a friend in Leo's plush romantic visions. The two signs conspire to become co-creators of a shared artistic process, finding the wellsprings of support to vulnerably expose whatever's being held close to their chests. Both loyalists to the core, durational partnership is a possibility, and as the zodiac's archetypal Mother and Father figures respectively, these two members of the same soul family can heal ancient wounds.

LEO: Leo-on-Leo action has all the makings of a sequined showstopper, as both parties take to the floor in their finest frocks. Both are lit by the never-ending belief in love after love after love. At its best and brightest, this dynamic duo can bring out the inherent generosity of spirit embedded in the sign. If they allow love to lift them up to where they belong, they can become cosmic cheerleaders of each other's every move. The key lies in remembering that there is always room for their twin flames, and they must work to stoke each other's specificity while soothing fears of being put out. When in doubt, letting stalwart support take center stage results in trampoline-sized leaps in mutual heart expansion.

VIRGO: An intricate union and ritualized affair, each can profoundly expand the other's trust in what they're here to contribute. Virgo's realism helps Leo hone its unending energy for creative participation in the world at large. And for Virgo, Leo's immediacy and obvious *joie de vivre* help soothe Virgo's hard edges, heating up a forgotten sense of play that doesn't need to be analyzed. They connect through a shared sense of integrity, bolstering their respective allegiances to unwavering inner sources of intuitive knowing. Together, their partnership is self-possessed and teaches both parties that they have the right to just be, in all their perfect imperfection.

LIBRA: Both visionaries in the sack, Leo and Libra seek romantic aspirations to tack to their mood boards. While Libra's intellectual approach can sometimes feel a little too minty cool for cinnamon-blooded Leo, at its best, this creative companionship can skyrocket both towards their greatest capacities for ideal love, with each acting as the other's perpetual artistic muse. Placing each other on pedestals is common, and both are urged to be careful about the inevitable fall. They must grow to accept each other in all their messy complexities rather than chipping away to create Greek-sculptural perfection.

SCORPIO: The only out-and-out carnivores in the zodiac, the appetites of this pair are insatiable, and sexual expression can reach deliciously sordid heights. Even in friendship, there can be something feverously frisky about this duo, as they erotically co-conspire about their next carnal pursuits or swap locker room stories about last night's conquest. The capacity for soul-deep transformation through collision is profound. If both stay open to clear negotiations of power and demonstrate their unending affection straightforwardly to soothe suspicion, they can take each other to emotional depths and developmental heights previously unimagined.

SAGITTARIUS: This larger-than-life collision is perpetually decked out in the oversized baubles of a love that liberates both of these fire babes from the mortal coil they long to leave behind. Fueling each other's sometimes-manic fires and self-scripted mythologies, the key can be learning how to stoke the flames without getting consumed in the carnal candle. While Sag's notorious need for ever-expanding horizons may threaten the little love cat's sense of loyalty, the wide-open vistas of the zodiac's wild pony can teach the kitten a thing or two about a love without borders. Leo learns to trust in holding a Sag's heart when the Lion learns not to keep it under lock and key.

CAPRICORN: Both embodiments of the archetypal "father figure," this paternalistic pair ignites themes of power, authority, and self-sufficiency. With Leo sometimes playing the eternal child to Capricorn's buttoned-up headmaster, the key to happy cohabitation lies in learning to protect rather than parent one another. No matter their walks of life, both of these signs have a penchant for opulence and an inherent desire to take to the throne of their own majestic birthright. Together, sensual indulgences can be a source of liberation, helping to build a shared belief in their diamond-encrusted worthiness.

AQUARIUS: On an oppositional polarity together in astrology, this pair can magnetize across a crowded room. They are co-conspirators in the search for unapologetic self-expression. The learning for this potent pair lies in the question of attachment, with the Leo forever pulled by its heartstrings and the Aquarius singing a tune crafted straight from its cerebellum. Aquarius' panned-out gaze helps draw Leo out of their sometimes self-centric experience, and the kitten's fluff and buff reminds Aquarius that they must have a heart beneath it all. Together, the duo comes ever closer to their shared vision of using their singular creative forces to light up the planet.

PISCES: A partnership that coaxes Leo into the silk sheets of its most sparkly dream life, this duo is all soft-lit romantics and mystical healing. Both parties' urge to escape into each other's arms is amplified, and if the pair commits to mixing their cloud life with some reality checks, the resulting relationship can bring heaven to earth. Leo gives structure to Pisces' loose edges, reminding the fishy that they have a right to ask for what they want directly, without a trace of shame. And Pisces beckons Leo into the deep end, soothing the Lion's endless appetite for ego expression and helping the love cat grow an everlasting trust in their specialness that never needs to be proven.

LEO

at Work

One of Leo's greatest longings is to gift their heat to as many plants as possible, watching flower petals open wide to greet their regal rise. And their capacity to spread this seed of sun-kissed selfhood can find magnanimous manifestation in their professional pursuits. More than any other sign, Leo must come at their careers heart-first, redefining the phrase "passion project" and collapsing the work/life divide. And as with all things Leonine, the question of fulfillment lies in harnessing the spark of their specialness to shine all the way to the back of the filing cabinet. They tend to do best when they feel confident that what the world needs now is more of the selves they already are.

Believing that they've been "chosen" to execute a mission bequeathed upon them by their personal god, Leos must commit to the credo that they were put here on the planet for a signature songwriting experience. This sign is encouraged to consistently create from the professional place that feels the most instinctively "true," cultivating a relationship of self-driven rightness that may fly in the face of external markers of success. If a Leo isn't coming into the boardroom completely alive and fully lit, they may as well have called in sick. No matter what professions they choose, Leos must follow their heat at all costs.

When they seem to have lost their connection to this career god, the key for the working Leo lies in holism. The Leonine obsession with authenticity finds both challenge and promise in the workplace as they seek to craft creative continuity between every piece of their glittering lives. Not ones to adopt a work persona that wouldn't be recognizable off duty, Leos shouldn't be afraid to exercise their right to match their life in the sheets with their work in the streets. They can find career ease by doing away with professional packaging and shedding the uniforms and suits cramping their styles.

And when their personal lives and professional pursuits find alignment, there's no other being that can light up a creative conference quite like a Leo. Aspiration, inspiration, and appreciation must travel hand in hand for these love cats. They will find balance through the feedback loop of personal dreams and collective needs. Impassioned speakers, inspired actors, and cosmic cheerleaders for their most downtrodden colleagues, Leos are here to transform glass ceilings into circus tents, reminding the rest of us that the journey to "make it" in the material world should be fueled by the magic of a profoundly personal mission.

FOLLOW THE SUN: CHOOSING A PATH

Like all fire signs, Leonine beings are lit from the inside out. They're invited to chart their career course from an inner code and concept rather than from the predetermined path society may have pushed them towards. Deciding a path must be born of pure desire, and wherever they find themselves on their journey of professional unfolding, Leos are urged to divine their guiding concepts first before getting mired in the specificity of skill sets.

When searching for a job or looking to renew their relationship to their current career, a Leo gets lit by choosing emotional rallying cries over already-posted job descriptions. Starting any job search by stating what they are here to bring to the world will ensure that their Leonine labors are truly connected with their luminous life forces. Stating something as simple and potent as "I am here to bring the romance" or "I want entering the office to feel like sinking my toes into the sand" will lead them closer to their career destinies. The panned-out, tagline portion of their resume is always more vital than the specific accomplishment details. Function should follow the feline form.

From the time they are wee ones, Leos cultivate strong aversions and attachments, and even seemingly innocuous hobbies and interests can dictate their career paths. It's not uncommon for a tiny Leo who spent hours smoothing Barbie locks to become a stylist, or for a sommelier to emerge from afternoons sniffing juicy fruits in the back-yard. When feeling lost, a Leo is always asked to return to these early images and sensory experiences when their heart first opened up. They must study the poetic traces of these life worlds to ensure full body and spirit alignment with their chosen path.

And while there certainly isn't an established list of careers that Leos should or shouldn't embrace, the key to crafting a purposeful path lies in the concept of customized creation. Whether it's a bespoke piece of parsley placed atop a cafeteria dish or tiny initials carved on the underside of an assembly-line item, Leos must know that whatever they're making in the world bears some resemblance to their own specialness. Whatever their line of labor, Leos are invited to find the mythos in the mundane and trail their glitter through even the most corporate halls.

BEDAZZLED DESKTOPS: LEO'S PROFESSIONAL STYLE

As the cosmos' party-ready playmate, the muted tones of duty can present a particular set of challenges for the Leonine spirit. Whatever their chosen path, their professional environment must feel like a kind of artist studio, and the laboring Leo is encouraged to transform their workspace into a living, breathing mood board. This space should spill over with personal flair to keep the flames lit. In even the most rigid of corporate dress codes, ensuring that a pair of undies or a tucked-away pendant is personally chosen provides Leos with an anchor of authenticity that keeps their core self secure and ready to find creative flow.

For Leonine beings, their work, like the rest of their

lives, is a constant act of creation and re-creation. Once established in a given role, the Leo both longs to lord over their lair, secure in their sense of competence, and perpetually prowl, chasing the next ambitious hit like a cat in heat. This is the paradox of "potential" that Leos will dance with all of their professional lives. They grapple with the roller-coaster concept of success and seek to define a custom-cut inner code to guard against the fear of perceived failure. Many Leo laborers will memorialize a particular creative high, convinced that they will never again be able to reach this professional pinnacle. And at the other end of the professional party pool, some Leos will remain in a role that's not as regal as they're worthy of out of fear that, by putting their full selves on the line, they might lose it all. In either case, there's a kind of high school football-star quality that can afflict career-driven Leos. They cling to the remembrance of championships past, which leaves them ravenously hungry to relive that one moment of stadium-sized magic.

To grapple with these swings between perceived potential and bottomed-out loss, Leos are invited to develop a sense of unshakable personal pride. Early on in a job, the love cat is tasked with creating their own form of performance review that exists outside the confines of their so-called superiors. Developing a kind of self-possessed "safe word" can return them to center during moments of professional turmoil. Whether it's a selfie they love tucked under their desk or a mantra as simple as "I am worth it" whispered under their breath, Leos must become their own authorities and acknowledge themselves first before seeking out external accolades.

When feeling satisfied with their own work, Leos transform into artistic visionaries perpetually greenlit by hot red passion. They can be delightfully playful thinkers, content to let the future unfold from the present. In brainstorming sessions, they splash around for the sheer joy of possibility. And when focused on an end goal, they tirelessly labor to realize their professional desires, outlasting many of their cosmic colleagues through their life force alone. As long as Leos can see a part of themselves reflected in what they produce, the labor is reward enough, and a Leo will fall in love with whatever career creature pops out.

WET 'N' WILD WATER COOLERS:
THE LEO COWORKER

The Leonine dream is a kind of perpetual Employee Appreciation Day, with Leo standing at the ready to receive a new Girl Scout patch or holiday bonus. When they can gift this sense of accomplishment to themselves, their potential to lift up their cosmic colleagues is immeasurable.

Leos often find themselves in leadership roles, fueled by seemingly unending sources of heat that others instinctively gather around. And as much as Leos long to feel their personal distinction, they can transfer this passion for particularity to others by inquiring about the bios and flavor palettes of each member of their work force and rallying each to surpass their own goals. As with any Leo in a position of power, Leo leaders are cautioned to "lift" rather than "lord over." At every step, they must ensure that their vision is fit to serve and be served by the whole, and they need to pay careful attention to the specific sparkle of each team member. And even if they don't bear the literal title of boss, Leos should always embrace their place and play their passionate part to the hilt, letting the contours of their turf keep the creative fires alight.

While fire can sometimes consume people who want to get close to its warmth, Leonine light is meant to be shared. Generosity grown through teamwork is highly encouraged. In the workplace, Leos can find themselves in fierce competition with their coworkers. If left unchecked by collaboration, this may lead to hungry grasping for turf. To combat this potential career cannibalism, a Leo should commit to growing their capacity to receive criticism. They must check in with core motivations to notice when attempts to swallow an effort through singular possession are actually stifling the joys of creation.

Leos are encouraged to explore the energetic concept of "ghostwriting" in their teamwork, learning to relish their individual contributions to the soup while also sitting back to savor the deliciousness of the full meal. Growing towards their "opposite" sign of Aquarius in the workplace will serve a laboring Leo well, and they're asked to experiment with gifting their creative efforts to a larger whole. This professional generosity allows them to see the shining faces of their colleagues as they experience the aftereffects of Leo's labors. When Leos strive to become Secret Santas instead of showstoppers, they'll be surprised at the delight produced by the precious presents they release into the wide world.

ALL THAT GLITTERS: MAKING MONEY

Like its fellow fixed signs (Taurus, Scorpio, and Aquarius), these kittens have incarnated to explore the concept of value, both inside and out. Rather than sweaty efforts to have and hoard, Leos learn to magnetize their gold through the sheer force of their own goldenness. Over the course of their professional pursuits, Leos are asked to probe this relationship between being and earning. Money must be the natural result of their creative impulses, rather than raison d'être. And when these high rollers are in full flow and immersed in their own pleasure process of making what's aligned with their heartbeat, the emerald oceans will open wide.

As Leos earn, they're consistently called to check in with their sense of deservedness, paying attention to moments when their desire to amass wealth or accolades borders on "lack" mentality. When feeling unworthy or unloved, the professional Leo can develop an envious streak that feeds on a sense of fundamental unfairness. In these moments,

Leos tend to focus on others who seem to somehow "have it all." Most Leos secretly harbor a desire for a full life of leisure. They want to stretch their paws out on the couch and wait for the next platter of treats. In times of financial fear or spiteful hedonism, a Leo is always encouraged to return to sweetness. They have to realize that they are their own greatest treasure, and there's nothing wrong with them loving up on their presence like a precious diamond.

Whether or not a Leo appears particularly glamorous on the surface, they often harbor dreams of a lavish lux lifestyle. Rather than dampen these desires or dismiss them as superficial, Leos are encouraged to deeply enjoy the fruits of their labors and let the juice drip down their chins. Experiencing ample, full-bodied pleasure always paves the way to securing sustainable wealth. Licking the plate clean and savoring the feeling of their bodies sliding into newly purchased pieces of clothing like second skins lets them see the shiny dazzle of their inner world made material in all its majesty. By bringing their entire presence to this process of spending, Leos fuel trust in the very realness of their contribution.

6

LEO

in School

As the love cat packs up its superhero lunchbox and sets off towards the halls of knowledge, their lifelong dance with themes of leisure, ambition, contribution, and distinction is amplified in the academic realm. For the fluffball tucked behind a grade school desk or burning the midnight oil in a college dorm, there will always be an inherent tension between the desire to be noticed, complete with sparkly superlatives, and the urge to find greater golden ease. The Leo student is forever in search of the creative flow that aligns their hearts with the juiciest apples of external assessment. They seek to earn gold stars for their very essence.

In elementary and middle school, Leos discover the delights and frights of lining up for roll call. They puff up their chests as they hear their names said out loud, wait with anticipatory dread for teams to be chosen, and seek their own reflections in the shiny stickers that may bedazzle their folders, papers, or lockers. A Leo will often adopt a special "persona" early on, embracing even the teasing of youth to remain apart, safe in the knowledge that even ridicule can be harnessed as a form of regality. A young Leo may also choose their own nickname at this juncture, and authority figures are urged to take this nomenclature seriously, as the Leo tends to brand itself early and for life. On the playground, Leos find their raison d'être. They harness the potential of these moments of unstructured abandon and use them to inject their studiousness with extra sparkle. The depth of their need for the release of recess is directly related to their capacity to get in formation.

As Leos approach the high school hallways, the urge to stand out and apart is further heightened, and whether it's the role of prom queen or rebel with a celestial cause, a Leo will find a way to stay on top by earning a special status. They are just as likely to become class president or captain of the football team as they are to be the one whispered about in locker rooms with a blend of adoration and fear. Teen Leo craves crafting their very own reputation. At this stage, the Leo student also starts to delight in the self-chosen sensuality that's beginning to blossom behind the bleachers.

They are fueled equally by the amorous adoration of teen romance and the promise of academic success.

If they choose to continue their education, Leos can truly come alive on college campuses, merging their ambitions for success with the greater freedoms of creative expression. At college, they can also blend their desire to do well with their deep *joie de vivre*. No matter how wild a Leonine collegiate gets, they somehow still manage to summon the firepower necessary to show up to their 8am. Thus they are able to savor their status as both party animal and star-kissed student. After college, continuing-ed Leos are urged to remain limber and open, as time can sometimes calcify this sign into a hard-contoured "know it all." But the late-in-life Leo learner can also find the fullness of their creative expression, deciding their very own curriculum with abandon and voraciously chasing the tail of every subject they've ever loved before it's too late.

CREATION STORIES: THE LEONINE MIND

Connected to the "intuitive" function, all fire signs are built to grasp the gestalt, sensing an inherent meaning in the world that transcends the rational. Swapping out questions of "what" and "how" for the elusive answer to "why," these signs simply have to believe that we're here for a purpose. The fervor of this oracular search for significance connects fire signs directly to their very reason for being: to bolster the belief that life, and thus their lives, can never be accidental. Finding meaning in the mundane gives them faith that they can "make things happen" and can actively pen their own autobiographies in turn. The specificity and secret life of every speck in a pile of dirt becomes evidence of their own specialness.

Less pragmatic and concrete than cardinal Aries and less philosophically or esoterically transcendent than Sag, Leo sits at the center of the BBQ, capturing the corner on fire's sense of fantasy and self-made mythology. Leo's mind literally looks for the light, seizing on subject matter that supports their sun-kissed credo, whether it's the happy ending to a fairy tale or the avoidance of the hard facts in a cold case that seem dehumanizing to the emo fluffball's tender heart. No matter their proclivities towards the "provable" subjects of math or science, there is always something of the poet inside the Leo learner. This instinct seeks to use flourishes and flowers to render even the most solid subject matter passionately personable.

Learning for Leos is always a process of self-study, and their penchant for poetics transforms any studious Leo into a lover fueled by a desire to see themselves reflected in the eyes of their chosen subject. However strange it may seem, Leo wants to feel like what they're learning is looking back at them with equal excitement. The mysteries of the universe seem to come alive in real time for Leos, as though knowledge itself were an after-hours library performance meant only for them. Knowledge, like beauty, is truly in the eyes of the beholder for Leo, who works tirelessly to track the heat of whatever subject has looked back at the love cat with amorous eyes. As a result they tend to favor information that supports their own notion of who they are.

TRAPPER KEEPER DREAMS: LEONINE STUDY HABITS

While the notorious Leo capacity for drama may find its way into explicitly performative subject matter, Leos don't need to take to the stage to seek out the full-color learning experiences they crave. Adding a heightened sense of narrative to fixed subjects is an act of the highest intellectual order. Personalizing the process thus helps Leos retain knowledge, especially when it comes to mundane learning environments. Adding bits of flair to their flashcards is always encouraged, as is harnessing their notorious animism to bring the world of learning alive. Turning rocks from geology class into precious pets, imagining the dating profiles of the periodic table's elements, or drawing lips and eyes on algebraic equations makes Leo an active participant in the artistic process of learning.

For the Leo to foster fervor for learning, they have to retain their authorial right to design the curriculum. Pouring over a course catalogue should feel like planning an elaborate vacation or selecting a gourmet meal. Assessing their agendas from a place of vibrant craving rather than externally imposed constriction helps Leos feel like they're in the intellectual driver's seat. Even for young Leos, having the power to choose their library books or the colors of their folders gives them a sense of self-defined meaning. Leo students of all ages are urged to exercise authority in ways that feel self-expressive. This helps ensure they don't act out in other areas of their academic lives. Simple things like stickers on a notebook or a signature swoosh as they shoot baskets in gym class can help Leo play the game.

Although Leo learning styles may vary, there's always something of the sensual kinesthetic in the love cat. They're always ready to immerse themselves in the process of rubbing up against the world to figure out what it's all about. While Leos may find some of the comfort they crave in more sedentary study sessions, complete with snacks and fluffy pillows of course, embodying knowledge is where Leos can best bring their subjects alive. When in doubt, a Leo learner is called to value the human over the heady, as they experience whatever they're reading about through a heart-shaped lens. Whether it's googling book authors for hours to understand their life stories or inspecting a plant outlined in a field guide, real-life, anthropological infusions help Leos find the closeness to the curriculum that they crave.

As a fixed sign, initiating a project can sometimes seem

daunting, and even the most studious Leo might sit in wait as a plan incubates, longing to pop out an entire castle in all its perfection before a single brick has even been laid. Leos can become paralyzed by both visions of greatness and despair, and although they have a penchant for big-picture thinking, their study habits improve when they simply choose a place to start and throw themselves in, which allows them to sense the heat and find the poetry in even the most minute movements forward. Celebrating all successes (regardless of size) in the unfolding of a project helps remind a Leo to embrace the good-enoughness of the present.

And while a Leo can dive deep and tunnel down into specific subjects, the key to their learning always lies in favoring full-bodied feelings over facts. Leos are asked to be extra-attentive to the information that ignites their instinctual participation. They should follow the lead of the topics that connect them to the larger-than-life mythologies that course through their bloodstreams. Focusing first on the emotions sparked by their studies liberates Leos to embrace the most customized creative path, no matter the academic requirements.

GOLD STARS: AMBITION AND ASSESSMENT

As the kings and queens of the jungle, the inherently hierarchical structure of schooling can strike a chord with the Leo student. They long to both participate, proving their worthiness in this lineup of laboring students, and self-assess their specialness, dancing out of the line to show the rest of the world that their scholarly prowess can't be tamed. The very notion of "standardized testing" flies in the face of Leo's belief in their specialness, which is anything but standard. During their academic growth, Leos must examine where their powers lie and carefully balance inner worthiness and outer assessments.

If given the opportunity, a Leo can truly thrive in Montessori school settings or other learning environments where the pure lusciousness of sharing knowledge takes precedence over linear grading. Self-assessment coupled with peer review can be a particularly fruitful combo for Leos. They learn to explore how they're received in the world without blocking out criticism and how to receive themselves more fully, no matter the outside rubric. In any assessment process, Leos are encouraged to focus on the quality of commentary instead of numerical marks, responding more to the narrative of what others feel about their work rather than a rigid mathematical rubric.

When placed in more traditional environments where scores and rankings are inevitable, Leo's penchant for prowess can burn out of control. As with all things Leonine, the high highs and low lows can infuse their studies with intense stakes, and the Leo student who feels they've "failed" can fall particularly hard. In these more challenging moments, Leos are urged to return to their potential for being fully present. To help soothe the hurt, they're asked to consider a single test question they answered with particular brilliance or focus on the sensation they felt when they learned something new.

Each sign in the zodiac serves as a kind of course correction and further flavoring of the one that precedes it. In school, Leos can learn a lot from their Virgo astro-neighbors. Balancing their exuberant forms of expression with Virgo's more humble, refined apprenticeship can help Leos navigate fears of failure and wild swings towards outsized greatness. While their natural proclivity may not be to follow, Leos are encouraged to sample subject areas that aren't immediately easy breezy. When they sample these more challenging subjects, they're asked to relish the release of just being, even if it means not being the best and the brightest. And it's when Leos let themselves relinquish the tireless call to climb on top that they can unleash their potential for generous encouragement, rallying their classmates towards intellectual exploration and cerebral play without judgment. By letting themselves remain in process, alternately adopting the give-and-take roles of teacher and student, expert and newbie, a true Leonine legacy of lifetime learning is forged.

LEO

in Daily Life

The word "daily" itself can bring on the doldrums for a Leonine queenie. They are forever searching for the highs of the haute life, even if they appear ascetic on the outside. Secret royalty resides inside of every Leo, whether the Glitter Kitten is harboring hopes of high-roller status or simply craving an artful dollop of cream on their everyday espresso. Leos seek majestic meaning and mythos that lift them far above the minutiae. And the golden nugget for navigating their dusk-to-dawn lies in saturating the quotidian with pomp and circumstance, no matter the occasion.

The guide below is intended as a primer on how to best navigate the rites and rituals of Leo's everyday, which entails keeping body and soul in alignment with the magic they came here to cast. It also includes some sensory suggestions for exploring what Leonine energy actually *feels like* on a visceral level, no matter the personal choices of the love cat in question. For example, the Leo call to cultivate over-the-top exposure might feel similar to spending a weekend at a Neoclassical-kitsch Vegas casino.

Luscious, vibrant, and expansive, this is meant to be a bedazzled deep-dive into the Leo lifeworld, complete with ruffled bikinis and cracked-open coconuts.

THE LION'S DEN: HOME DÉCOR

Fellow fire signs Aries and Sag can easily live out of a duffel. Aries is content stripping off the extraneous and foregoing any sense of place in favor of sheer force, and Sag is perpetually in motion and always prepared to jet into the sunset. In contrast, as a fixed fire sign, Leo craves a good curl-up by the hearth. And whether the love cat is stuffed into an overcrowded apartment like a little cream puff or all alone in a backwoods lair, there is something sumptuous and capacious they're seeking as they create a nest.

In any home setting, starting with the principle of sensuality is paramount. When a Leo goes shopping for home goods, they must run their hands over the fabrics and rub their cheeks against the pillows. Similar in energy to fellow fixed sign Taurus, they are tactile beings, longing for closeness with the edge of every table and wrapping themselves in silk sheets in order to buff and shine their inner lights. Stabilized through softness, Leos can cultivate more of their call to come at the world heart-first through furniture that feels plump and plush. Faux fur always wins out over bare wicker. Throws and rugs of the sheepskin variety are particularly fetching for the feline. They provide lasting leisure and serve as places to splay out. They can also be used as makeshift capes for when Leos want to pretend they are royalty.

No matter the architectural confines of their homes, the feline floor plan is an invitation to explore the concept of self-presentation. The emphasis is on foyers, landings, and fridge doors, which all serve as opportunities for Leo to construct a sense of self. Keeping a bouquet of bodacious blooms on the hall table reminds Leos of the generous potential of self-expression. They learn to prize an ego that warms all those who enter, and instead of blaring into the beings of friends and family, they leave a subtle scent. Coffee tables and kitchen counters are also sites of self-construction, and a Leo is encouraged to carefully consider what objects sit atop these altars. They should take personal pride in turning these shared sites into living mood boards. These parts of the home serve as literal reflections of Leo's selfhood, helping to stabilize any grasping need to "prove" their identity.

And whatever their décor preferences, to experience Leonine home energy to the hilt is to take cues from the palatial kitsch of Liberace, Vegas casino lobbies, and Graceland, or the bombastic cupcake stylings of Rococo. There's an earnestness to the opulence in these environments. A kind of democracy exists among all the unique embellishments and exuberant, stylistic celebrations coming together. In these kinds of habitats, Leo can uncover a playful sense of regality. They claim their thrones carefully, but with unapologetic camp, bursting through the boundaries of "good taste" to savor a more-is-more mentality that all but banishes minimalism.

CROWN JEWELS: PERSONAL STYLE

A Leo's body is an extension of their very soul. For no other sign is the question of personal style more critical. Whether they're fashionistas or minimalistas (and even the most ascetic Leo has a streak of maximalism lurking somewhere inside), embodied presentations must be artful and aligned with an authentic knowledge of themselves. Adornment is the guiding light for a Leo in the dressing room. The act of draping and cloaking becomes a kind of personal love letter written by Leo to Leo.

For Leos, beauty is much more than skin deep, and whatever their personal style proclivities, self-expression starts at the vanity table. In fact, the more elaborate the beauty ritual behind the scenes, the fuller and more fit the Leo feels to enter the world. These private rituals can boost the Leo's confidence and get them feeling more like their true selves. Luxurious night creams and body oils are favored. They allow the Leo to care for the special contours of their skin and give themselves the tender touch they long to receive from the world at large. Adopting a beauty regimen can help elevate their autobiographical aesthetics. They can imagine themselves as stars in the pages of a classic Hollywood glossy describing the intricacies of their favored routine. And no matter the look, Leo's crowning jewel is literally their crown. Whether they've gone full-on Rapunzel or are buffed bald, there's always something of the Texan credo "the higher the hair, the closer to God" about their heads. Leos are encouraged to care deeply for their coiffure with curl creams, beard oils, or simply some sunscreen if they're sporting an exposed melon.

Leaving a trail of paw prints as they travel the world, Leos are invited to play with adopting a signature scent with strong sillage. Entering a room through an olfactory trace before they're officially there, or lingering on the exit, can help Leo believe they are potent and significant. Their coterie should be able to pick them out of a crowded room without even seeing them, and their signature scent should make them unforgettable. No matter the nose, the literal "scent" of Leonine energy can be found in gourmand fragrances that burst into being. Such scents are doused in the heady aromas of an edible bouquet made of roses and chocolates. At its most straightforward, the scent of Leo is suntan lotion. This lotion's explosion of coconuts, papayas, and tropical fleurs matches the sign's straightforwardly sunny credo.

When choosing their clothing, Leos are urged to scrap the fashion mags and forge their own path. The too-trendy Leo is always a sign that the Lion has, in some sense, lost their way. In these closet cases, eschewing dress codes in favor of a personally threaded destiny will bring them back to creative center. Even the most conservative cat is invited to find some piece of signature flair, whether it's a ripe cherry lip to offset a neutral work suit, a power color (preferably some variety of cocktail shade—think Bahama Mama coral or Blue Hawaii turquoise), or a proprietary silhouette that they always sport. The quintessential Leonine fashion energy is a hybrid of John Waters's camp, Vegas showgirl, and '80s prom, complete with Lisa Frank rainbow leopard prints, hot pink gloss, and oversized gemstones fit to be licked. Achingly tender and gaudily gorgeous, Leo style hits its stride when it's self-chosen and aligned with the kitten's agenda to turn even the stuffiest closet into a celebration.

FANCY FEASTS: DIET AND HEALTH

The Leonine palate is always somewhat hedonistic, and whatever they choose to snack on must feel distinctively fun, with multiple courses and extra toppings to prolong the flavor party. For even the most solitary cat, communal eating can be a balm to their generous souls, especially when they're the invited guest and not the chef. When feeling blue, Leos are encouraged to head out into the world for a mini feast. Losing themselves in the bustle of a crowded urban market of splashy delectables, or indulging in piling the buffet platter high, helps remind Leos that the world is still worth snacking on.

To help bolster their trust in their undeniable, uncomplicated essences, Leos are invited to explore flavors that are deliciously straightforward. Mediterranean cuisines are a prime example of Leo's sun-soaked fullness and capacity for simple holism. Squeezing a fresh lemon into sparkling water, dipping a toasty baguette into extra-virgin olive oil, or sucking on the salty, savory skin of a Greek olive reminds the love cat of the purity of the present moment, nourishing their spirit through luxury that doesn't have to be overly complex. Whatever their particular health plan, occasionally indulgent, rich foods are to be celebrated. Sometimes they simply need to choose creamy butters, say yes to dessert, or, if they're so inclined, delight in an after-dinner digestif. Leos need to be lotioned from the inside out, and like all fire signs, the Lion's appetite can come on with ravenous immediacy. Warm, sustaining meals help stretch the Leo towards the sun, and sitting down for an epic, Spanish-style dinner should always be chosen over the furtive handful of dried fruit grabbed on the go.

Leos well-being centers around a healthy heartbeat. Of all the fire signs, Leo loves sedentary sumptuousness the most. This can create the need to get "circulating," so the kitten must occasionally tear itself from its patch of sun and chase something sparkly in the name of cardiovascular health. But any Leonine fitness regime must feel like self-adornment. Kitten carnality is sparked by the promise of pleasure as much as an end goal of diamond-cut abs. Exercise should contain something of the "epic" about it, and even if the Leo won't end up literally performing a dance number, any workout set to cinematic soundtracks will help Leo to see contouring their physical body as an act of self-creation.

In playing with various shades of ego expression, Leos are invited to choose sweat-drenched pursuits that both open them to the gaze of another and allow them to keep something for themselves. A prime example of this process can be found in pole-dancing classes and sensuous floor work, where a Leo can rub up against hard surfaces and literally use their body to transcend the boundaries of a room. With an audience, they inevitably see their own reflection, and they're asked to uncover the auto-erotic in this process. In any style of dance class, Leos are invited to experiment with the mirrors, swapping between gazing straight into their own eyes and looking away. This practice helps them build contentment and trust in what happens to their forms when they can't see what's happening. Partnered dance classes can be particularly supportive, as the Leo learns to follow cues from another, releasing into the give-and-take of being held and seizing the lead. Synchronized swimming is another prime opportunity for Leo to both shine and blend. They can burst out of the water on occasion for a signature leap, but most of the work happens anonymously, while they're among their fellow water babes.

THE LION AT REST: LEISURE PURSUITS

Set to a constant soundtrack of Leo-queen Madonna's "Holiday," there's a leisurely thread that pervades all aspects of the Lion's life. Whether working late at the office or buried in beach sand, Leos are invited to sink their toes into the available ease in every moment, relaxing their bodies into a breezy beingness with the world around them. And when it's actually time to out-and-out play, Leos are urged to go full force, forgoing working vacations and skill-centered leisure pursuits for the ecstasy of pure, unadulterated pleasure. Off-duty experiences are an opportunity for Leos to completely banish any notion of "shoulds," and when selecting their leisure activities, the sign is encouraged to always choose celebration over "self-betterment."

Hobbies for the Lion must be ripe with hot-blooded passion, and even a pottery class can spark secret sensual scenes from the movie *Ghost*. If they've got a penchant for producing crafts, a Leo is encouraged to choose more abstract artistic expressions in which they can let loose and liberate their own creative choices. Rather than signing up for an elaborate needlepoint class or carefully knitting a sweater, the love cat is beckoned towards bigger canvases, choosing mural painting or sculpture making instead. Retaining innocence in their pursuits is the key to lasting happiness, and when in doubt, Leos are encouraged to return to the simple acts that sparked their hearts as youths. Whether it's pouring over vintage toys on eBay or deciding that their hobby is lying on a blanket in the sun, leisurely Leos are encouraged to bring their full presence to even the smallest moments. They shouldn't be afraid to gift themselves the full glory of their own bodies in repose.

If traveling to a more exotic location, the Leonine spirit craves a piña colada experience. Their energy best aligns with tropical islands and dream vacations. Cruises, all-inclusive resorts, and Vegas-style weekends are the ultimate Leonine celebrations, as they support an "all you can" abundance mentality, a nowhere-to-go sense of constancy, and a dazzling, showtime energy of endless entertainment. And whether or not the Leo is an actual beach babe, hot-blooded locales are emblematic of the jungle cat's essence. Whether it's Hawaii, the Caribbean, Miami Beach, or the French Riviera, a Leo getaway should carry the golden keys to the honeymoon suite, complete with ceiling mirrors and a heart-shaped tub.

COSMIC CAT CALENDAR:
A LEONINE YEARLY PLANNER

Follow the activations below to find your flair in every season . . .

★ Ruled by the icy peaks of Capricorn, January urges Leos to slough off any excess and return to their simple majesty, seizing their birthright as feline queens.

★ Electrically charged by change maker Aquarius, February encourages Leos to mix their passion for the present with some fantasy future tripping.

★ The end of the astrological year, March's Piscean vibes let Leos loosen their grip and embrace more allowing, favoring pool floatie freedoms over ferocious self-protection.

★ The astro year's Aries spark plug, April asks Leos to consider how to streamline their singular force, only putting their prints on projects that make their hearts beat faster.

★ Sprawled out and sumptuous, May's Taurus-ruled bounty of blooms reminds Leos that they have every right to receive whatever pleasures they want to paw.

★ June's Gemini-governed breezes invite the love cat to taste the rainbow, swapping some of their tightly held convictions for the curious sensation of windsock wonder.

★ Ruled by Little Mermaid Cancer, July is high tide for Leos to return to the private parts of their creative process, as they learn to balance stepping out with the serenity of their inner sanctum.

★ The heart of Leo's birth season, August is a catcall to come to the party with ruffles and without reservation, and Leos are asked to get even more touchably tender.

★ Wrapped in the witchy, ritualistic arms of earthy Virgo, September requests Leo's full embodiment, ushering the kitten to listen to the subtle signals of their physical form.

★ Watched over by crystal-clear Libra, October proposes Leonine partnership pacts, as the love cat learns to balance their ego expression with careful acts of caring compromise.

★ Injected with the no-holds-barred intensity of Scorpio energy, November begs Leo to remember their boldness, letting the fur fly in the face of any fears about being "too much."

★ Home for the holidays on a Sagittarius saddle, December ushers Leos back to the love bounty, reminding the jungle cat of their generous mission to gift even more of their light.

8

LEO

in the World

The Leonine legacy looms large in the world, and these big, fluffy cats are notorious for leaving their creative marks in neon lights and Walk of Fame paw prints. Whether it's their personal or workaday personas, the larger Leo destiny must always seek to align inner passions with outer flames, connecting their power moves to their very personhood at all costs.

A PLACE IN THE SUN:
LEAVING A LEONINE LEGACY

Leo's fire energy connects us to the hearth. It's a living embodiment of how to feed the flames for the collective while also keeping the self toasty-warm. Fittingly, Leonine forays into the world at large start with a commitment to their own private wellsprings of courage. Behind-the-scenes prep in the dressing room is vital to building trust in the self and helping to soften the bumps from the big bad world.

Preparing for any flavor of public foray carries this call

for personal and collective integration, and Leos are urged to create a kind of energetic "anchor" to keep their inner flames moored and stoked as they're pushed and pulled by the external. This can be a kind of love locket—an imagistic memory or projection of a special moment where they succeeded or felt in deep alignment with the flow of life. Or it can be quite literal, such as carrying a signature candle to hotel and conference rooms as an embodied reminder of what is most essential to their soul in pre-performance moments.

During this process of preparing to step out and encounter the world, Leos are encouraged to adopt some form of "power pose" before they leave the house. For example, they could flex before a mirror to remind themselves of their own strength. Encountering their body in the silence of solitude helps bolster Leo's inner sources of confidence and prevents situations where they have to "puff up" unduly as they enter the world. And if hands-on-the hips superhero stances seem too silly, Leos are encouraged to prep for their global entries through subtler means, such as applying lotion to their legs with concentrated attention or rolling in the sheets to a favorite slow jam.

More than any other sign, Leos are invited to pay attention to the relationship between their cultivated personas and their behind-the-scenes lives. They are asked to work to close the divides and coax their selfhoods from out behind any obscuring screens. No matter how explicitly performative a given Leo is, they must concentrate on stabilizing their identity and understanding exactly who they are, what they're here to give, and how they're received. Even the realest Leo will put a mask on sometimes, seeking adoration over authenticity and losing a little bit of self-love and true light in the process. The answer, as with all things Leonine, lies in following their heat maps of passion back home. Leos are literally stamping the world and bringing their inner essence out. And while this is certainly replete with its challenges, Leos have to learn to practice what they preach. Magnetizing a lasting legacy lies in first attempting to come at the world boldy unmasked and beautifully bare skinned.

TALL TAILS: PRIMA DONNA PATRON SAINTS

While the list of Leonine heroic hedonists and signature survivors is long, these five feline friends best embody Leonine principles.

MADONNA (8.16.58): The songs of Ms. Ciccone read like a literal bible of Leonine sparkle and flair. From the unapologetic opulence of "Material Girl," and the hot-blooded hedonism of "Erotica," to the full-hearted presence of "Cherish," and the tenderly innocent "Like a Virgin," Madonna's catalogue charts the Leonine principle of heat. The original "Express Yourself" songstress is a poster queen for both the jungle cat's prowess and the house cat's pop-tastic purrs.

CARL JUNG (7.26.1875): A deep lover of the language of astrology, this Swiss psychoanalyst was given over to archetypal imaginings and art-based therapies. One of the first people to define the concepts of introversion and extroversion (the very essence of the Leonine dance between inside and out), Jung found fiery meaning in even the most mundane happenings. Paying homage to the significance of synchronicity and the mysteries of consciousness, his approach underlines the lovable human behaviors that exist far beyond logic.

HARRY POTTER (7.31.80): Created by fellow feline J. K. Rowling (with the same DOB as Harry, but in 1965), the legacy of this little light worker rests in aligning desire with destiny and soothing performance anxieties by trusting in his inherent gifts. Left with a pot of wizard's gold to navigate the world, and a leader in the house branded by the Lion, Potter must reckon with all parts of his essence, both golden and shadowy. As he defends his magic with honor, he learns to trust in his own sense of right and wrong above everything.

BARACK OBAMA (8.4.61): The 44th president embodies the Lion's principles of exposure and potential, breaking the historical molds to risk creating a heart-centric legacy in a land built on linear success. Whatever your political thoughts on the specifics of affordable health care, Obama's lasting trail through the halls of history was no doubt blazed on the belief that we all deserve to have a shot at shining our light.

SCRATCH 'N' SNIFF: FINDING LEO IN THE LANDSCAPE

The hermetic incantation "as above, so below" reminds us that astrology isn't just an out-there system of distant stars and predestined outcomes. Instead, this sensuous language lives and breathes, speaking to us of our participation in nature and the material world. Bringing heaven to earth, astro energies are everywhere, and discovering them can feel much like being out on a treasure hunt. They are found in everything from the dirt (related to Taurus and Scorpio root system energies of grounding down and digging in) to the sky above (Aquarius and Libra vibes of high-minded idealism and critical thinking). Here are some celestial scavenger-hunt sites to encounter the bombastic Leo babe out in the big old world.

SUMMERTIME: Whatever your hemisphere, Leo energy burns most brightly when the sun is at its peak, a veritable "high noon" of the cosmos. Wherever heat is found, Leo is lurking, and stepping out into solar landscapes is the most immediate means to powering up with the energy of this sign. The principle of "seamlessness" is strongest here, when you're literally stripping down to your skin to experience the closeness of the weather. While Leo energy can polarize into the performative, at its most vital, it is connected to essence and the innocence of the skinny-dipping suits we sport as we greet the sun.

RIPENESS: The physical sensation of biting into a plump peach or juicy tomato and letting it stream down your chin is a visceral experience of over-the-top Leonine pleasure. The same is true of the willingness to let our unstoppable essences spill over the edges of propriety. In the process of ripening, there's also a connection to the creative act in all its skin-exposed sensitivity. As we play with harvesting the literal fruits of our labors, we learn when something is ripe and ready for the world and when it needs further incubation. Most importantly, we learn how to care for ourselves through the tender process of blooming.

CATS: The most obvious symbol of Leonine fluff and flair, these beautiful beasts carry the Leonine paradox of wildness and civilization, best observed in their muscular tails. In both jungle and house varieties, there is a deep penchant for possession. They draw their prey and their precious ones close with dug-in claws. In the wild, lions are "hyper-carnivores," sinking their teeth into a diet consisting almost entirely of meat. On the softer side, purring is a highly developed hormonal release that heals pain. It's tied to Leo's work expanding the concept of strength to include tenderness. Whether tucking into a kitty cup or roaming the land as the leader of a pride, their sensitive whiskers and ravenous lust for life make them perfectly equipped to rule their lairs with majesty.

CHILDREN: Whether it's a petulantly personal tantrum or the wide-eyed glory of playground presence, Leo energy can always be accessed through youth. A kind of real-time narration invites young people into the flow of life, curiously reaching out to connect through the constant asking of questions or the voicing of immediate needs without shame. Although Leo is traditionally associated with ages 28–35, when the foundations of a lasting sense of self are tested and tried, an even deeper core self is forged in our earlier fantasy years. They are proof that we all have a right to relish the wisdom of our inner wee one.

COLOR: Leonine energy is full-spectrum and full-on, and whenever you catch a glimpse of a super-saturated shade, trust that Leo energy is powering up this palette for your delight. The Leonine invitation to match our soul's true colors with our advertised shade is embodied in the rainbowness of nature, as animals and plants sport coats that flash warning signals or come-hither throbbings. And you don't have to travel deep into the wilds to find Leo. It can be encountered at your local hardware store or beauty shop. Look for this sign's showstopper glow in paint samples, crayons, and lusciously lickable lip gloss.

POP MUSIC: Whatever your feelings about chart-topping ear candy, there's something distinctly Leonine about the magnanimous melodrama and emotional democracy of songs you can karaoke to with unabashed glee. Leo energy is here to remind us that cynicism and hardness can leave us dry and brittle while earnest innocence lubricates our mission to love again. Even in the throes of heartbreak, Leonine vibes are still open and humming. They dress up even their sadness in pink poofs. Close your eyes, pump up the jams, and lose yourself to the sweet sensation.

CONCLUSION

Now that you've brushed up against all the bedazzled facets of this sun-scorched feline fluffball, it's time to take it to the streets. Whether you're a Leo Sun sign who's looking to renew their commitment to their personal mission or simply an aficionado craving more Leonine light in your life, follow the energy checklist below to power up your fiery force.

HEAT. *When do I feel the sensation of complete warmth? What triggers this feeling?*

EXPOSURE. *What does it feel like when I show myself completely? When I hide instead, what am I protecting?*

REALNESS. *What am I made of? What would it mean to become more of this?*

SPECIALNESS. *What is my signature? What is the one thing that only I can bring forward?*

CREATION. *What wants to come through me? What is my personal definition of success? How can I support my own birthing process?*

PLAY. *How can I return to an absolute innocence that lights me up from the inside out? When do I feel alive without strategy?*

PRESENCE. *Am I ready to risk trusting this life completely? What does it feel like when I'm simply here, now? What parts of my life, and which people in it, can I accept exactly as they are?*

PLANETARY PAWS: LEO IN YOUR BIRTH CHART

Whether or not you were blessed to be born under the Sun sign of the kitten, Leo light is for everyone. Here's how to feel the heat, no matter your sign.

Leo Planets and Personal Placements

When you look up your birth chart, you'll discover that you're not just your Sun sign. Rather, you are composed of an array of celestial cuties, each symbolizing a different part of your life force and personal cosmic story. First, explore if you have any other planets or placements in the sign of Leo.

LEO RISING: The Rising is the kind of packaging we arrive in. It indicates the energy of our approach (the lens we use to view the world) and calls on us to take this sign's principles to a deeper level. Leo Rising signs are invited to show up in every sense of the phrase, syncing their inner and outer presentations on a more profound level.

MOON IN LEO: The moon is a tucked-in shellabration of our inner worlds. It's symbolic of how we feel and what makes us secure. For Leo Moons, emotions run high and can't be hidden, as the sun is literally shining through the moon and sporting its heart on its sleeve. Stability is found when they learn to lick their own wounds, which then enables them to give even more of their generous hearts.

MERCURY IN LEO: Quick-footed Mercury is the zodiac's butterfly, ruling perception, communication, and how we relate to everyday change. Mercury in Leo uses words to delight and dazzle, enamored of its personal poetics and custom credos. Opening up to more varied viewpoints is a growing edge. This placement is asked to learn the art of adaptation, rather than always firmly anchoring.

VENUS IN LEO: Pleasure-petaled Venus rules all kinds of receiving, from money to food to sex. It describes how we "take in" the world, content to magnetize rather than force our mojo. In fiery Leo, the ante is upped for adoration, and this sign placement craves heavy petting and fixed attention. Growth comes from accepting the inevitable ups and downs of love and seeing objects of affection as more than just materials.

MARS IN LEO: Mars is our red-hot muscle and mojo, the source of both our sexuality and success drive. In Leo, the engine revs are related to the heart-center, and passion projects are an absolutely vital source of sustenance. These jungle cats are also learning to trust in their irreplaceability. They're still figuring out that they no longer need to sing for their fancy feast—the world will come to them.

JUPITER IN LEO: Jupiter is the planet that blows open our windows and doors, beckoning us to expand beyond our constrictive beliefs and risk connecting to our wild natures.

In Leo, the party rages on, and this sign placement is both gifted with an ability to land forever sunny-side up and asked to bring greater consciousness to its personal definition of true happiness.

SATURN IN LEO: Saturn is the planet of limits and laws, a sometimes hard-knocks school that paves the way towards lasting competence. In Leo, there can be a kind of school-yard push and pull between the urges to play and self-critique. With effort and attention, Leonine exuberance can break free, and this sign placement's secret superpower lies in birthing creative projects through pragmatism.

URANUS IN LEO: This rule breaker and change maker shakes it up, interrupting our usual societal programming and urging us to travel beyond the mapped roads. Uranus in Leo is a living, breathing embodiment of originality, here to reshape the very concept of identity and risk eccentric expression to rally the troops.

NEPTUNE IN LEO: A generational planet that shifts signs every 14 years, Neptune is the zodiac's dream queen, an escape hatch that takes us into the mystical world and symbolizes where we crave transcendence. Neptune in Leo builds faith through force, bowing at the altar of creative expression and personal significance.

PLUTO IN LEO: The outermost generational "planet," Pluto is ruler of the underworld, a jet-black metal detector indicating where we must enact karmic change. In Leo, self-expression is associated with incredible intensity and high stakes. With this Pluto placement, family legacies may have to be explored so that we can unearth whether or not our specialness is truly being supported.

CHIRON IN LEO: This touchy-feely planetoid is ready for healing. It asks us to develop deep sensitivity and awareness in its sign placement without expecting immediate fixes. In Leo, there's a tenderness connected with fully and vibrantly just being us—a call to develop deeper compassion in regard to our very natures.

NORTH NODE OR SOUTH NODE IN LEO: The Nodal axis connects us to past lives and future promises, as we're asked to integrate both our North and South Node signs to come closer to our soul's purpose. With one of the Nodes in Leo, and the other in Aquarius, the work lies in balancing between the heart and the head, and in understanding both individual expression and collective participation.

No planets stamped by the love cat? Read on to learn how you can still access Leonine flair. . .

The House Ruled by Leo

Check out the pie slices of your chart and look for the Leo symbol. This is the arena of life in which you're invited to enjoy a Leonine approach. Over time, you'll cultivate greater trust in its contents and learn to savor its tastiness.

The Sign Ruling the Fifth House

The fifth pie slice is naturally ruled by Leo, and as the house of "creation and re-creation," it symbolizes the artistic process and all shades of romance. Whatever sign you have here is key to unlocking your birthing potential. It governs how you fall in love, raise your children, shape your creative clay, and find faith in your particular flavor of self-expression.

Your Sun Sign

Literally ruled by the sun, Leo energy reminds us that we are all custom-built stars on a personal mission to sign our hearts on the dotted line. Whatever your Sun sign placement, it's here where you're meant to shine. Consider it both a marker of what you already are and an unfolding destiny you're asked to dynamically develop.

Leo Season

As the sun travels through the entire zodiac, it spends about a month in each astrological sign. Each of us has the opportunity to celebrate and integrate these twelve powerful archetypes. As Leo season dawns in late July and August, it's a heightened invitation for everyone to leap back onto the dance floor, claim our true colors, and shimmy with the sweet knowledge that all we have to do is become more of what we already are.

INDEX

LEO

ABOUT THE AUTHOR

BESS MATASSA is a New York-based astrologer and tarot reader with an Aries sun and a fluffy little Leo moon. After completing a PhD, she went rogue and started bringing heaven to earth through customized cosmic experiences ranging from birth chart walking tours to zodiac perfume-making classes and tarot dance parties. She is the co-author of *The Numinous Astro Deck* (Sterling, 2019), the author of *Zodiac Signs: Virgo* (Sterling, 2020), and has been a cosmic consultant for brands and platforms including *Teen Vogue, PureWow, Apartment Therapy,* and Almay cosmetics. Bess serves up mystical self-inquiry with a side of play, poetry, and pop music, harnessing the language of the cosmos to bring us deeper into the vivid world that surrounds us and the luscious, lovable selves we already are.

ABOUT THE AUTHOR

BESS MATASSA is a New York-based astrologer and tarot reader with an Aries sun and a fluffy little Leo moon. After completing a PhD, she went rogue and started bringing heaven to earth through customized cosmic experiences ranging from birth chart walking tours to zodiac perfume-making classes and tarot dance parties. She is the co-author of *The Numinous Astro Deck* (Sterling, 2019), the author of *Zodiac Signs: Virgo* (Sterling, 2020), and has been a cosmic consultant for brands and platforms including *Teen Vogue, PureWow, Apartment Therapy*, and Almay cosmetics. Bess serves up mystical self-inquiry with a side of play, poetry, and pop music, harnessing the language of the cosmos to bring us deeper into the vivid world that surrounds us and the luscious, lovable selves we already are.

OTHER BOOKS IN THIS SERIES